The Plutarch Project Volume Four

(Revised)

Demosthenes, Cicero, and Demetrius

by

Anne E. White

ISBN: 978-978-1-990258-14-5

CONTENTS

Introduction

These notes, and the accompanying text, are prepared for the use of individual students and small groups following a twelve-week term.

The text is a free mixture of Thomas North's 1579 translation of Plutarch's *Lives of the Noble Greeks and Romans* and John Dryden's 1683 translation. (Dryden for clarity, North for character.) Omissions have been made for length and suitability for the intended age group. Those using audio versions or other translations will want to preview those editions for "necessary omissions."

Some lessons are divided into two or three sections. These can be read all at once, or used throughout the week.

Using the Introductory Material

Each study contains explanatory material before the first lesson. The parent/teacher should examine this before beginning the study, and choose when or how to present the material. A little at the beginning of the first lesson may be useful to stir interest in the study, but it is not meant to be given all in one dose! The information may help as you introduce later lessons, or to answer students' questions.

I encourage you to make the lessons your own. Use the discussion questions that are the most meaningful to you. Remember that Charlotte Mason was satisfied with "Proper names are written on the blackboard, and then the children narrate what they have listened to." She also emphasized the importance of recapitulation, which can have two meanings: beginning each lesson by remembering what has gone before, or recalling something already known; and emphasizing particular points at the end of a lesson, which (again) should help with the next one.

Examination Questions

These studies include suggestions for end-of-term examination questions. The questions for *Demosthenes* were drawn from original PNEU term programmes; the others were written for this book.

Special note for this volume

The *Life of Demosthenes* is, for Plutarch, unusually brief: it takes up 32 pages in North's translation, compared with 53 pages for *Cicero* and 60 for *Demetrius*. That makes the lessons short, and there are only ten of them. If you need material to fill the extra weeks in a term, here are two suggestions:

1. Do the study of *Cicero* first, then *Demosthenes*, and read Plutarch's comparison at the end. (The text is included at the end of *Demosthenes*.)

2. Use the extra time for creative narrations, including debate, recitations, or speeches. The following activity is suggested for **Lesson Three**, but could be done any time: "Demosthenes preferred to have his speeches planned out, but some of his hearers said that his off-the-cuff orations were better. For fun (or as a serious exercise), prepare and deliver a short speech. Then have someone suggest another topic for you to speak on without preparation. Which was easier for you? Which talk did your audience enjoy more?"

Demosthenes

(384-322 B.C.)

"Demosthenes affects no learning; he aims at no elegance; he seeks no glaring ornaments; he rarely touches the heart with a soft or melting appeal, and when he does, it is only with an effect in which a third-rate speaker would have surpassed him...The secret of his power is simple, for it lies essentially in the fact that his political principles were interwoven with his very spirit." (*Harper's Dictionary of Classical Antiquities*, 1898)

The World of Demosthenes

The Golden Age of Athens lasted from 480 B.C., with the end of the Persian Wars, until 404 B.C. and its defeat in the Peloponnesian War. The Athens into which Demosthenes was born barely resembled its former self. At one time, Athens had ruled an empire; now most of its ships had been destroyed, and its young men killed or imprisoned. Still, life went on, and the city attempted to improve its economic health and re-establish its democratic government. But even greater threats to its survival were soon to come from the northern kingdom of Macedonia.

Is it Macedon or Macedonia? Were the Macedonians Greeks?

The names are used interchangeably. Macedonia, or Macedon, was a kingdom in the northeastern part of mainland Greece. The Macedonians were Greek in many respects, such as religious beliefs; but they valued their distinct heritage and identity

How was Athens ruled in the fourth century B.C.?

If you have read Plutarch's *Life of Nicias*, you will remember the Sicilian Expedition of 415-413 B.C (during the Peloponnesian War). Because of that defeat, the government of Athens was taken over by an **oligarchy** (a small group of rulers); but that was soon replaced by a more democratic form of government, which remained in place (with occasional interruptions) until Macedonia took control in 338 B.C.

What is a commonwealth?

A commonwealth can refer either to one state, usually a democratic republic; or to a state plus its associated territories or colonies (its extended family, so to speak). In this story, the **commonwealth** refers to Athens and its dependencies (other places under its protection and control).

Who was Demosthenes?

Demosthenes was not a military leader (as demonstrated by his behaviour during battle); nor was he an elected official. He was an orator; a philosopher; a public prosecutor and defender, and a political analyst. As a defender of Athenian liberty, he talked his fellow citizens into allying themselves with other cities (such as Thebes) to resist the Macedonians.

"Philip and Alexander"

Some students will already be familiar with these two Macedonian kings, father and son. For those who are not, it is important to view the life of Demosthenes in the context of their reigns: first, because his life covered almost exactly the same years as theirs; but, second, because he became known for his impassioned speeches against them (the **Philippics**). (**Word Trivia:** Because of Demosthenes, a **philippic** came to mean any vehement, bitter speech against someone.)

What was the Third Sacred War?

Plutarch refers several times to this war (356-346 B.C.), but he calls it the War of/with the Phocians (the people of **Phocis**, not to be confused with **Phocion**, the Athenian general). The war started out as a conflict between Greek states, but ended up involving Macedonia as well, and the Macedonians jumped at the chance to increase their power. After almost ten years of fighting, the Athenians were planning to send a military force to help the Phocians, but the Phocians suddenly asked for a peace settlement. This is the point at which Athens, seeing that its own security could now be threatened, also sent a delegation to ask for peace terms (**Lesson Four**).

Who was Demades?

Demades was an Athenian orator who was about the same age as Demosthenes. At first he supported Demosthenes, but later they became enemies because of their different visions for the future of Athens. Demades was taken prisoner by the Macedonians at the Battle of Chaeronea, but made such a good impression on King Philip II that he was released, and he helped create a peace treaty between Macedon and Athens (**Lesson Seven**). This was good for his own popularity, but it didn't help the worsening public opinion of Demosthenes. He was, eventually, responsible for Demosthenes' death sentence.

Other orators we should remember?

> **Phocion:** an Athenian statesman and *strategos* (general), and the subject of one of Plutarch's *Lives*. He did not care for long-winded speeches, and Demosthenes called him "the axe of my words" (**Lesson Three**).

> **Pytheas:** the orator who told Demosthenes that his speeches "smelled

of the lamp" (**Lesson Two**); he was also the prosecutor in the Harpalus case (**Lesson Eight**).

Why are there only ten lessons in this study? *(Repeated from the introduction to this volume)*

The *Life of Demosthenes* is, for Plutarch, unusually brief: it takes up 32 pages in North's translation, compared with 53 pages for *Cicero* and 60 for *Demetrius*. If you need material to fill the extra weeks in a term, here are two suggestions:

1. Do the study of Cicero first, then Demosthenes, and read Plutarch's comparison at the end. (The text is included at the end of Demosthenes.)

2. Use the extra time for creative narrations, including debate, recitations, or speeches.

"Is This Going to be on the Exam?"

As noted, the story of Demosthenes is short, but that does not make all of it easy to understand, especially when Plutarch skips quickly over information that may be new to students. There are a lot of names in this story (including historical sources), and a lot of places to search for on maps. The focus is on Athens, but the increasing power of Macedonia is also important. A point worth bringing up during this study is that the insubordination of Athens, though irritating to Philip and Alexander, was by no means their only or biggest concern. Greece was only one piece in the planned worldwide empire of Macedonia.

However, at least in the single P.U.S. term we know of in which Demosthenes was studied (Programme 107), the examination emphasis was almost wholly on his character, and on the ways he used his oratorical skills. It may be read largely as a study of the responsibility that those with a public voice have to speak plainly and honestly (as much as is humanly possible), and the equally important role played by those who listen. It is also a story that acknowledges human temptations and failings, even of those who have earned public admiration.

Therefore, while there are certainly interesting rabbit trails in this story, teachers and students may both need occasional reminders that it really is all right not to have the full back story on every king or general; it is fine just to have a general idea of some of the places. Try to keep the focus on Demosthenes himself, and you will be fine.

Top Vocabulary Terms in the *Life of Demosthenes*

If you recognize these words, you are well on the way to mastering the vocabulary for this study. They will not be repeated in the lessons.

1. **countenance:** face; facial expression

2. **disposition:** temperament, character

3. **drachma (pl. drachmae or drachmas), mina(s), talent(s):** units of money. A mina was originally equal to 70 drachmae but it was later raised to 100. A talent was a large amount of silver or gold.

4. **eloquence:** skill in public speaking, especially in pleading a case or persuading people to do something.

5. **meet:** suitable, proper

6. **orator:** a professional public speaker. At this time, orators often used their gifts to make political speeches, or to defend or accuse someone in court (the word **pleader** is also used in this story).

7. **periods:** sentences

8. **preferred:** proposed

9. **pulpit for orations:** speaker's platform; rostrum

10. **rhetoric**: the formal art of persuasion or motivation through public speaking or writing. A **rhetorician** can be an orator, or a teacher of that art (or both).

Lesson One

Introduction

Plutarch, in an unusually personal introduction, talks about some of the difficulties he has in trying to write biographies "from materials gathered by observation and the reading of works not easy to be got in all places, nor written always in his own language, but many of them foreign and dispersed in other hands," especially because he did not live in a place with great libraries or other resources. He then introduces Demosthenes and Cicero: "two orators…who, from small and obscure beginnings, became so great and mighty." (Cicero is the subject of the next study.)

Vocabulary

happy: When Plutarch says that **happiness** is something "placed in the qualities and disposition of the mind," he relates it closely to **virtue**. Christian students may want to compare this with the word translated "blessed" or "happy" in the Beatitudes (Matthew 5).

requisite: necessary

virtue: moral (and overall) excellence

ingenuous: This word is often used now to mean sincere and innocent, even naïve; but in earlier times it meant noble, honourable.

industrious: hard-working

thoroughly inhabited: with a large population

deficient: lacking

in my latter time: in my old age

commonwealth: see introductory notes

confer their works and writings of eloquence: Dryden says "to criticize their orations one against the other" (the thing he does not intend to do)

contested with: fought for power against

trial of skill: contest, competition

did let the rest run to naught: they mishandled the money

liberal sciences: academic subjects such as philosophy

forbore to urge him: refused to push or force him

meagre: scrawny

enervated: nervous, stammering

give himself to eloquence: become an orator

Oropos incident: Callistratus had recommended that the Athenian-Theban quarrel over **Oropos** (a disputed border town) be settled diplomatically; but when the plan failed, he and another orator were brought to court to defend themselves.

bore the bell: had the highest reputation

People

Sosius: Quintus Sosius Senecio was a Roman senator and consul in the first century A.D., whose literary friends included Pliny the Younger and Plutarch. Some of Plutarch's other writings refer to conversations that had taken place in both Greece and Rome, and it appears that Sosius even attended the wedding of Plutarch's son.

Alcibiades: Athenian statesman of the fifth century B.C.; the subject of one of Plutarch's *Lives*.

Euripides: a writer of tragic plays

Caecilius: Caecilius of Calacte, a literary critic and historian

Theopompus: a Greek historian

Callistratus: (or Kallistratos); Athenian orator and general

Isaeus: an Athenian orator

Isocrates: a famous teacher of rhetoric

Historic Occasions

404 B.C.: End of the Peloponnesian War

384 B.C.: Birth of Demosthenes

382 B.C.: Birth of Philip II of Macedon

On the Map

General introduction: For this study you should have access to a historical map of **Greece** and its surroundings, showing it as it was during the fourth century B.C. A map or pictures of **Athens** (and its region **Attica**) would also be helpful. You will want to note the surrounding bodies of water (including the **Mediterranean** and the **Aegean** seas), and the various city/states such as **Thebes** and **Corinth**. If the students have not done much study of Greece before, they should learn or review the general geography, e.g. the near-separation of the north and south (the **Peloponnesus** or **Peloponnese**) at the **Isthmus of Corinth**.

Oropos: a small town in east Attica, formerly controlled by Athens, but at this time by the **Thebans**

Reading

Prologue (A general introduction to Demosthenes and Cicero)

Whoever it was, **Sosius**, that wrote the poem in honour of **Alcibiades**, upon his winning the chariot race at the Olympian Games (whether it were **Euripides**, as is most commonly thought, or some other person), he tells us, that to a man's being **happy** it is in the first place **requisite** he should be born in "some famous city." But for him that would attain to true happiness, which for the most part is placed in the qualities and disposition of the mind, it is, in my opinion, of no disadvantage to be of a mean, obscure country [*omission*]...for **virtue**, like a strong and durable plant, may take root and thrive in any place where it can lay hold of an **ingenuous** nature, and a mind that is **industrious**.

I, for my part, shall desire that for any deficiency of mine in right judgment or action, I myself may be, as in fairness, held accountable, and shall not attribute it to the obscurity of *my* birthplace.

But if any man undertake to write a history that has to be collected from materials gathered by observation, and the reading of works not easy to be got in all places, nor written always in his own language, but many of them foreign and dispersed in other hands: for him, undoubtedly, it is in the first place and above all things most necessary to reside in some great and famous city **thoroughly inhabited**, where men do delight in good and virtuous things, because there are commonly plenty of all sorts of books, and upon inquiry may hear and inform himself of such particulars as, having escaped the pens of writers, are more faithfully preserved in the memories of men, lest his work be **deficient** in many things, even those which it can least dispense with.

But I myself, that dwell in a poor little town, and yet do remain there willingly lest it should become less: whilst I was in Italy, and at Rome, I had no leisure to study and exercise the Latin tongue, as well for the great business I had then to do, as also to satisfy them that came to learn philosophy of me; so that even somewhat too late, and now **in my latter time**, I began to take my Latin books in my hand. And thereby, a strange thing to tell you, but yet true: I learned not, nor understood matters so much by the words, as I came to understand the words by common experience and knowledge I had in things. But furthermore, to know how to pronounce the Latin tongue well, or to speak it readily, or to understand the signification, translations, and fine joining of the simple words one with another, which do beautify and set forth the tongue: surely I judge it to be a marvellous pleasant and sweet thing, but withal it requireth a long and laboursome study, meet for those that have better leisure than I have, and that have young years on their backs to follow such pleasure.

Therefore, in this present book, which is the fifth of this work, where I have taken upon me to compare the lives of noble men one with another: undertaking to write the lives of Demosthenes and Cicero, we will consider and examine their nature, manners and conditions, by their acts and deeds in the government of the

commonwealth, not meaning otherwise to **confer their works and writings of eloquence**, neither to define which of them two was sharper or sweeter in his oration. The which **Caecilius**, little understanding, being a man very rash in all his doings, hath unadvisedly written and set forth in print, a comparison of Demosthenes' eloquence with Cicero's. But if it were an easy matter for every man to know himself, then the gods needed have given us no commandment, neither could men have said that it came from heaven.

The divine power seems originally to have designed Demosthenes and Cicero upon the same plan, giving them many similarities in their natural characters: as, both of them to be ambitious, both of them to love the liberty of their country, and both of them very fearful in any danger of wars. And likewise their fortunes seem to me, to be both much alike. For it is hard to find two orators again, who, from small and obscure beginnings, became so great and mighty; who both **contested with** kings and tyrants; [who] both lost their daughters; [who] were driven out of their country, and returned with honour; who, flying from thence again, were both seized upon by their enemies; and [who] at last ended their lives with the liberty of their countrymen. So that if we were to suppose there had been a **trial of skill** between Nature and Fortune, as there is sometimes between artists, it would be hard to judge whether the first succeeded best in making them alike in their dispositions and manners, or the second in the coincidences of their lives.

We will speak of Demosthenes first.

Part One

Demosthenes, the father of this orator Demosthenes, was, as **Theopompus** writeth, one of the chief men of the city, surnamed the Sword-maker, because he had a great shop where he kept a number of slaves to forge them.

[omitted: brief speculation about Demosthenes' parentage]

His father died when Demosthenes was seven years old, and left him reasonable well: for his goods came to little less than the value of fifteen talents. Howbeit his guardians did him great wrong: for they stole a great part of his goods themselves, and **did let the rest run to naught**, as having little care of it, for they would not pay his schoolmasters their wages. And this was the cause that he did not learn the **liberal sciences** which are usually taught unto honest men's sons: besides that, on account of weakness and delicate health, his mother would not let him exert himself, and his teachers **forbore to urge him**.

He was **meagre** and sickly from the first, and hence he had his nickname of "Batalus" given him, it is said, by the boys, in derision of his appearance; Batalus being, as some tell us, a certain **enervated** flute-player, in ridicule of whom Antiphanes wrote a play.

[omission: possible other meanings of Batalus]

Part Two

The occasion (as it is reported) that moved him to **give himself to eloquence**, was this. Callistratus the orator was to defend himself before the judges, regarding his actions over the **Oropos incident**; and every man longed greatly for this day of pleading, both for the excellency of the orator, that then **bore the bell** for eloquence: as much as for the matter, and his accusation, which was manifestly known to all. Demosthenes hearing his schoolmasters agree together to go to the hearing of this matter, he prayed his schoolmaster to be so good as to let him go with him. His master granted him, and being acquainted with the keepers of the hall door where this matter was to be pleaded, he so entreated them, that they placed his scholar in a very good place, where being set at his ease, he might both see and hear all that was done, and no man could see him. Thereupon, when Demosthenes had heard the case pleaded, he was greatly in love with the honour which the orator had gotten, when he saw how he was attended home with such a train of people after him: but his wonder was more than all excited by the power of his eloquence, which seemed able to subdue and win over anything. Thereupon he left the study of all other sciences, and all other exercises of wit and body, which other children are brought up in: and began to labour continually and to frame himself to make orations, with intent one day to be an orator among the rest.

His master that taught him rhetoric was named **Isaeus**,

notwithstanding that **Isocrates** also kept a school of rhetoric at that time: either because that, being an orphan, he was not able to pay the wages that Isocrates demanded of his scholars, which was ten minas; or because he preferred Isaeus's speaking, as being more business-like and effective in actual use.

[omission for length]

Narration and Discussion

How much does your birthplace, or the country or city where you live now, influence your character, or the opportunities you have? Why might you want to stay in the home town instead of living in a big city? But what are the advantages of the city, especially for a scholar?

Describe the early childhood of Demosthenes. What were the experiences that most shaped his later life?

For further thought: Would you prefer your oration to be sharper, or sweeter?

For older students: Can good character, or virtue, take root in even a poor environment if it finds an accommodating nature?

Creative narration: "Demosthenes hearing his schoolmasters agree together to go to the hearing of this matter, he prayed his schoolmaster to be so good as to let him go with him." Retell or act out this story in any way you choose.

Lesson Two

Introduction

This lesson begins one of the most well-known tales of Demosthenes' life: how he trained himself, through extremely hard work and against physical limitations, to become a great orator. (The story of him filling his mouth with pebbles does not appear until **Lesson Three**).

Vocabulary

to go to law with his guardians: to sue his guardians for the misuse of his **patrimony** or inheritance

he obtained it: he won his case

spleen: an abdominal organ, part of the immune system

lusty and nimble of body: physically strong and agile

the great garland games: athletic competitions at which the prize was a garland (vs. a larger reward such as money or olive oil)

cumbered: burdened, weighed down

impediment: a hindrance or obstruction

forsook the assembly: stopped attending public meetings

having a manner of speech…: this was a great compliment, as Pericles had been a much-admired Athenian statesman and orator

faint heart: lack of courage

suffering: allowing

had the hustings for their own: had the platform to themselves

without book: by heart

rehearsed: recited

exercise himself in declaiming: go to the trouble of making a speech

enunciation: pronouncing words clearly

without intermission: without a break

go abroad: go out and about

subservient to his studies: he used everyday conversation as his training material

peradventure: perhaps; by any chance

"smelled of the lamp": seemed overly rehearsed and artificial

briefs: notes

People

Thucydides: a Greek historian

Satyrus: an actor and friend of Demosthenes

Pytheas: see introductory notes

Historic Occasions

366-364 B.C.: Demosthenes delivered orations against his guardians

On the Map

Piraeus: As Athens did not have a harbour of its own, it made use of the one at nearby Piraeus.

Reading

Part One

As soon, therefore, as he was grown up to man's estate, he began **to go to law with his guardians**, and to write orations and pleas against them: who in contrary manner did ever use delays and excuses, to save themselves from giving up any account unto him of his goods and **patrimony** left him. And thus, following this exercise (as **Thucydides** writeth), it prospered so well with him, that in the end **he obtained it**, but not without great pains and danger; and yet with all that he could do, he could not recover all that his father left him, by a good deal. And having got a taste of the honour and power which are acquired by pleadings, he now ventured to come forth, and to undertake public business.

For, as there goeth a tale of one Laomedon, an Orchomenian, who having a grievous pain in the **spleen**, by advice of physicians was willed

14

to run long courses to help him; and that, following their order, he became in the end so **lusty and nimble of body**, that afterwards he betook himself to **the great garland games**, and indeed grew to be the swiftest runner of all men in his time; even so, the like chanced unto Demosthenes. For at the first, beginning to practise oratory for recovery of his goods, and thereby having gotten good skill and knowledge how to plead: he afterwards took upon him to speak to the people in assemblies, touching the government of the commonwealth, as if it were in the great games, and at length did excel all the orators at that time.

But when he first ventured to speak openly, the people made such a noise, that he could scant be heard; and besides, they mocked him for his manner of speech that was so strange, because it was **cumbered** with long sentences, and was so intricate with arguments one upon another, that they were tedious, and made men weary to hear him. And furthermore, he had a very soft voice, an **impediment** in his tongue, and had also a short breath, the which made that men could not well understand what he meant, for his long periods in his oration were oftentimes interrupted before he was at the end of his sentence.

So that, in the end, being quite disheartened, he **forsook the assembly**. As he was walking carelessly and sauntering about the **Piraeus**, an old man named Eunomus the Thriasian found him, and sharply reproved him, and told him that he did himself great wrong, considering that, **having a manner of speech much like unto Pericles**, he drowned himself by his **faint heart**, because he did not seek the way to be bold against the noise of the common people, and to arm his body to [do] away with the pains and burden of public orations, but **suffering** it to grow feebler, for lack of use and practice.

Part Two

Another time, being once again repulsed and whistled at, as he returned home, hanging down his head for shame, and utterly discouraged: **Satyrus**, an excellent player of comedies, being his familiar friend, followed him, and went and spoke with him. Demosthenes made his complaint unto him, that where he had taken more pains than all the orators besides, and had almost even worn himself to the bones with study, yet he could by no means devise to please the people; that drunken sots, mariners, and illiterate fellows were heard, and **had the hustings for their own**, while he himself was despised.

Satyrus then answered him, "Thou sayest true, Demosthenes, but care not for this, I will help it straight, and take away the cause of all this: so thou wilt but tell me, **without book**, certain verses of Euripides, or of Sophocles." Thereupon Demosthenes presently **rehearsed** some unto him, that came into his mind. Satyrus, repeating them after him, gave them quite another grace, with such a pronunciation, comely gesture, and modest countenance becoming the verses, that Demosthenes thought them clean changed. By this, being convinced how much grace and ornament language acquires from action, he began to esteem it a small matter, and as good as nothing for a man to **exercise himself in declaiming**, if he neglected **enunciation** and delivery. Hereupon he built himself a place to study underground (which was still remaining in our time); and hither he would continue, oftentimes **without intermission**, two or three months together, shaving one half of his head, that so for shame he might not **go abroad**, though he desired it ever so much.

Nor was this all, but he also made his conversation with people abroad, his common speech, and his business, **subservient to his studies**, taking from hence occasions and arguments as matter to work upon. For as soon as he was parted from his company, down he would go at once into his study, and run over everything in order that had passed, and the reasons that might be alleged for and against it. And if **peradventure** he had been at the hearing of any long matter, he would repeat it by himself: and would finely couch and convey it into proper sentences, and thus change and alter every way any matter that he had heard, or talked with others. Hence it was that he was looked upon as a person of no great natural genius, but one who owed all the power and ability he had in speaking to labour and industry. Of the truth of which it was thought to be no small sign that he was very rarely heard to speak upon the occasion, but though he were by name frequently called upon by the people, as he sat in the assembly, yet he would not rise unless he had previously considered the subject, and came prepared for it.

So that all the other orators would many times give him a taunt for it: as **Pytheas**, among others, that taunting him on a time, told him, his reasons **"smelled of the lamp."** "Yea," replied Demosthenes sharply again, "so is there great difference, Pytheas, betwixt thy labour and mine by lamplight." And himself also speaking to others, did not altogether deny it, but told them plainly, that he did not always write at length all that he would speak, neither did he also offer to speak, before he had made **briefs** of that which he would speak. He said furthermore, that it was a token the man loved the people well, that he would be careful before what he would say to them.

Narration and Discussion

How did Demosthenes' struggle against his guardians help him train for his career? Christian students may want to look up Romans 8:28, and think about how God uses even difficulties for good.

What were Demosthenes' weaknesses as a speaker? How did Satyrus inspire Demosthenes to improve his skills?

Creative narration: Choose a passage such as a Shakespearian monologue, a famous poem, or another piece of writing. Find an audio or video version of a professional actor reciting the same passage. How do the actor's skills bring the written words to life?

Lesson Three

Introduction

As Demosthenes improved his speaking abilities, he began to be compared with great orators. But, Plutarch says, it was "his own natural wit" that truly helped him succeed.

Vocabulary

timorous: timid, hesitant

inveighed: protested, complained

curry favour: try to gain favour by flattery or special attention

17

convey himself out of the assembly: sneak out of the room

the character of Pericles: Demosthenes had been told that his style of oration called to mind that of Pericles (**Lesson Two**); but he seemed to be less interested in using Pericles as his role model in other aspects such as character.

reserve: a formal, dignified manner of speaking, to the point of being aloof or unwilling to open oneself up to others

sustained manner: dignified, formal way of standing and moving

forbearing: restraining oneself from acting; holding back

premeditation: planning, forethought

transported into a kind of ecstasy: overwhelmed with emotion

without art: simply by using his natural gifts

invincible: unconquerable

long-studied reasons: careful preparation

"See, the axe of my words riseth": Dryden, "Here comes the knife to my speech."

bodily defects of nature: physical shortcomings

base and mean: ignoble, unrefined

People

Aeschines: an Athenian orator

Python of Byzantium: a Greek statesman who later represented Philip of Macedon in Athens

Lamachus, the Myrinaean: a sophist, which at that time meant a teacher or professor, especially of rhetoric

Philip and Alexander, kings of Macedon: see introductory notes

Eratosthenes: Eratosthenes of Cyrene, a famous scholar

Demetrius of Phalerum (c. 350-280 B.C.): Athenian orator and philosopher, who also appears in Plutarch's *Life of Demetrius*

Demades: see introductory note

Aristo [or Ariston] of Chios: a Stoic philosopher, teacher, and orator; nicknamed "The Siren" because of his persuasive speeches

Theophrastus: a philosopher

Phocion: see introductory notes

Historic Occasions

357/356 B.C.: The Third Sacred War began (see notes in the introduction to this study). Macedon captured two Athenian colonies (Pydna and Potidea).

356 B.C.: Birth of Alexander the Great

354 B.C.: Demosthenes made his first political speeches

352 B.C.: Demosthenes is believed to have made his first speech denouncing Philip

351-350 B.C.: First (official) Philippic

On the Map

Thebes (Thebans): a city in **Boeotia**, in central Greece

Olynthus (Olynthians): an ancient city of **Chalcidice** (in Macedonia)

Reading

Part One

But now might a man ask again: If Demosthenes was so **timorous** to speak before the people upon the sudden: what meant **Aeschines** then, to say that he was "marvellous bold" in his words?

Or, how could it be, when **Python of Byzantium**, with so much confidence, and such a torrent of words, **inveighed** against the Athenians that Demosthenes alone stood up to oppose him?

And how chanced it that **Lamachus, the Myrinaean**, having made an oration in the praise of **Philip and Alexander, kings of Macedon,** in the which he spoke all the ill he could of the **Thebans**, and of the **Olynthians**, and when he had read and pronounced it in the open assembly of the Olympian games: Demosthenes upon the instant rising up on his feet, declared, as if he had read some history, and pointed as it were with his finger unto all the whole assembly, the notable great service and worthy deeds the which the Thebans and Chalcidians had done in former times, for the benefit and honour of Greece?

And in contrary manner also, what mischief and inconvenience came by means of the flatterers, that altogether gave themselves to **curry favour** with the Macedonians? With these and such like persuasions, Demosthenes made such stir amongst the people, that the orator Lamachus, being afraid of the sudden uproar, did secretly **convey himself out of the assembly**.

Demosthenes, it should seem, regarded other points in **the character of Pericles** to be unsuited to him; but his **reserve** and his **sustained manner**, and his **forbearing** to speak on the sudden, or upon every occasion, as being the things to which principally he [Pericles] owed his greatness, these he [Demosthenes] followed, and endeavoured to imitate. And like as he would not let slip any good occasion to speak, where it might be for his credit: so would he not likewise over-rashly hazard his credit and reputation to the mercy of Fortune. And to prove this true, the orations which he made upon the sudden without **premeditation** before, do show more boldness and courage than those which he had written, and studied long before: if we may believe the reports of **Eratosthenes, Demetrius of Phalerum**, and the comical poets. Eratosthenes says that often in his speaking he would be **transported into a kind of ecstasy**.

[omission: some notes about Demosthenes' eloquence]

And yet everybody did grant, that **Demades**, of his own natural wit, **without art**, was **invincible**: and that many times speaking upon the sudden, he did utterly overthrow Demosthenes' **long-studied reasons**. And **Aristo of Chios**, has recorded a judgment which

Theophrastus passed upon the orators; for being asked what kind of orator he accounted Demosthenes, he answered, "Worthy of this city." Then again, how he thought of Demades: "Above this city," said he.

The same philosopher writeth also, that Polyeuctus the Sphettian (one of those that practised at that time in the commonwealth) was wont to say that Demosthenes was the greatest orator, but **Phocion** the ablest, as he expressed the most sense in the fewest words. And to this purpose, they say that Demosthenes himself said also, that as oft as he saw Phocion get up into the pulpit for orations to speak against him, he was wont to say to his friends: **"See, the axe of my words riseth."** Yet it does not appear whether he had this feeling for his powers of speaking, or for his life and character, and meant to say that one word or nod from a man who was really trusted would go further than a thousand lengthy periods from others.

Part Two

But now for his **bodily defects of nature**. Demetrius of Phalerum writeth that he heard Demosthenes himself say, being very old, that he did help them by these means. First, touching the stammering of his tongue, which was very fat, and made him that he could not pronounce all syllables distinctly: he did help it by putting of little pebble stones into his mouth, which he found upon the sands by the riverside, and so pronounced with open mouth the orations he had without book. And for his small and soft voice, he made that louder, by running up steep and high hills, uttering even with full breath some orations or verses that he had without book. And further it is reported of him, that he had a great looking-glass in his house, and ever standing on his feet before it, he would learn and exercise himself to pronounce his orations. For proof hereof it is reported, that there came a man unto him on a time, and prayed his help to defend his cause, and told him that one had beaten him; and that Demosthenes said again unto him, "I do not believe this is true that thou tellest me, for surely the other did never beat thee." The plaintiff then thrusting out his voice aloud, said: "What, hath he not beaten me?" "Yes, indeed," quoth Demosthenes then: "I believe it now, for I hear the voice of a man that was beaten indeed." Thus he thought that the sound of the voice, the pronunciation or gesture in one sort or other, were things of force to believe or discredit that which a man sayeth.

The action which he used himself, when he pleaded before the people, did marvellously please the common sort; but the noblemen, and men of understanding, found it too **base and mean**, as Demetrius of Phalerum said (among others). And Hermippus writeth that one called Aesion, being asked his opinion of the ancient orators, and of those of his time, answered that it was admirable to see with what composure and in what high style they addressed themselves to the people; but that the orations of Demosthenes, when they are read, certainly appear to be superior in point of construction, and more effective.

[omission for length]

Narration and Discussion

Demosthenes liked to plan his speeches ahead, but some of his hearers said that his off-the-cuff orations were better. Why was this so?

Can you think of times in the Scriptures when God gave people courage to speak, even against opposition?

For older students: In his first Philippic, Demosthenes said that "for a free people there can be no greater compulsion than shame for their position." What did he mean?"

Creative narration #1: For fun (or as a serious exercise), prepare and deliver a short speech. Then have someone suggest another topic for you to speak on without preparation. Which was easier for you? Which talk did your audience enjoy more?

Creative narration #2: Many people remember the story of Demosthenes and the pebbles, but not as many have heard this one: "And for his small and soft voice, he made that louder, by running up steep and high hills, uttering even with full breath some orations or verses that he had without book." Try it and see if it works!

Lesson Four

Introduction

So far, the story of Demosthenes has been about the ways in which he matured both personally and professionally. Now the story moves on to political events, particularly the relationship of Athens to Macedon.

Was Athens at war or at peace with Macedon, and when?

War and peace were complicated things at that time. Sometimes there were small wars (such as the "reducing of Euboea"); and sometimes there were bigger, longer wars against the same enemy, or with different allies. What we do know is that after some crushing Macedonian victories in 348 B.C., Athens sent a group of ambassadors (including Philocrates, Aeschines, and Demosthenes) to try to negotiate peace. This was Demosthenes' first meeting with Philip, and it was not exactly a friendly one, especially because Philip's proposed terms were harsh (forcing them to give up some territory). The ambassadors agreed, however, to accept the the terms, and sent another delegation soon afterwards to, so to speak, sign the contracts. When they arrived, Philip was out of the country, apparently seizing more territory before he could be charged with violating the treaty. Demosthenes wanted to track Philip down and force him to sign it, but the others voted to remain in Pella until he returned. Eventually the treaty (the "Peace of Philocrates") was signed, but only after great delays. And when, soon afterwards, the city of Phocis was taken, the Athenians did not even send help; they could not, under the peace terms they themselves had signed.

How does that history fit in with this lesson?

Plutarch moves back and forth in time in a way that may be confusing. He tells about the first peace embassy, but barely mentions the second one. What we do see clearly, however, are Demosthenes' efforts to unite the Greeks against this powerful (and devious) enemy—and to bring in as many extra soldiers as they could muster. But would that be enough to save Athens?

Vocabulary

Phocian war: see introductory notes for this study

Philippic orations: speeches that Demosthenes made against Philip of Macedon; see introductory notes

that action: the war

prevailing: winning his case

fickle: apt to change loyalties or opinions

prevaricate: tell a lie

were contemporary with him: lived at the same time

commendable: praiseworthy

mutiny: rebel

aristocratical: favouring the interests of the aristocracy rather than those of the common people

court of Areopagus: the supreme court in Athens

burn the arsenal: set fire to the city's dockyards (and ships)

one of the ten ambassadors…: see **Historic Occasions**

fair: nice-looking, handsome

pleader: a lawyer, pleading a case; or a sophist (see **Lesson Three**)

the reducing of Euboea: a battle against Philip on the island of Euboea, which ended in a stalemate (although Plutarch says that they "chased the Macedonians out of the island")

tyrants: local rulers

he brought them all into a general league: We will hear more about this in the next lesson.

strangers: mercenary soldiers; foreigners hired to serve in the army

People

Meidias (or Midias): a wealthy Athenian who became an enemy of Demosthenes, apparently because of a property dispute

king of Persia: this would be **Artaxerxes III**

Aeschines: see **Lesson Three**

Hypereides (or Hyperides): a speechwriter and orator

Melanopus: another orator

Callistratus: see **Lesson One**

Nicodemus the Messenian: a politician who shifted sides

Cassander: one of Alexander's successors who ruled Macedonia after his death

Demetrius: Demetrius I Poliorcetes, subject of Plutarch's *Life of Demetrius*

Ephialtes: an early leader of the democratic movement in Athens

Aristides: nicknamed "The Just"; general during the Persian Wars

Cimon (Kimon): Athenian statesman and general

Antiphon: There were orators by that name, but this particular Antiphon is known only for his traitorous act against Athens. Why did he offer to help the Macedonians by setting fire to the shipyards? Apparently he had been stripped of his Athenian citizenship due to some offense, and this was his retaliation.

Historic Occasions

348 B.C.: Macedon's crushing victories in the Chalcidice region made Athens decide to "sue for peace"

347 B.C.: Demosthenes was part of the delegation sent to **Pella** (in Macedonia) to discuss peace terms with Philip

346 B.C.: The Third Sacred War (Phocian War) officially ended, leaving Philip with great power over Greece.

340 B.C.: Philip besieged the cities of **Perinthus** and **Byzantium**

On the Map

Phocians: the people of **Phocis** (see introductory notes)

Susa and Ecbatana: important cities of the Persian empire

Reading

Prologue

Demosthenes' first entering into public business was much about the time of the **Phocian war**, as [he] himself affirms, and may be collected from his **Philippic orations**. For of these, some were made after **that action** was over, and the earliest of them refer to its concluding events. It is certain that he engaged in the accusation of **Meidias** when he was but thirty-two years old, and was of small countenance and reputation in the commonwealth: the want whereof was the chiefest cause (as I think) that induced him to withdraw the action, and accept a sum of money as a compromise. For of himself—

> He was no easy or good-natured man,

but of a determined disposition, and resolute to see himself righted; however, finding it a hard matter and above his strength to deal with Meidias, a man so well secured on all sides with money, eloquence, and friends, he yielded to the entreaties of those who interceded for him. But had he seen any hopes of possibility of **prevailing**, I cannot believe that three thousand drachmas could have taken off the edge of his revenge.

Part One

The object which he chose for himself in the commonwealth was noble and just, the defense of the Grecians against Philip; and in this he behaved himself so worthily that he soon grew famous, and excited attention everywhere for his great eloquence and plain manner of speech. Thereby he was marvellously honoured also through all Greece, and greatly esteemed with the **king of Persia**; and Philip himself made more account of him (Demosthenes) than of all the orators in Athens. His greatest foes, which were most against him, were driven to confess that they had to do with a famous man. For, in the orations which **Aeschines** and **Hyperides** made to accuse him, they write thus of him.

So that I cannot imagine what ground Theopompus had to say that Demosthenes was of a **fickle**, unsettled disposition, and could not long continue with one kind of men, nor in one mind for matters of state; whereas the contrary is most apparent, for the same party and post in politics which he held from the beginning, to these he kept constant to the end; and was so far from leaving them while he lived that he chose rather to forsake his life than his purpose. He was never heard to apologize for shifting sides, like Demades, who would say he often spoke against himself, but never against the city; nor as **Melanopus**, who, being generally against **Callistratus**, having his mouth stopped many times with money, he would go up to the pulpit for orations, and tell the people, that "indeed Callistratus, which maintaineth the contrary opinion against me, is mine enemy, and yet I yield unto him for this time: for, the benefit of the commonwealth must carry it."

And another also, **Nicodemus the Messenian**, who being first of **Cassander's** side, took part afterwards with **Demetrius**, and then said that he did not speak against himself, but that it was meet he should obey his superiors. We have nothing of this kind to say against Demosthenes, as one who would turn aside or **prevaricate**, either in word or deed. There could not have been less variation in his public acts if they had all been played, so to say, from first to last, from the same score.

[omission of more in the same vein]

Certainly amongst those who **were contemporary with him**, Phocion, though he appeared on the less **commendable** side in the commonwealth and was counted as one of the (pro-)Macedonian party, nevertheless by his courage and his honesty procured himself a name not inferior to these of **Ephialtes, Aristides**, and **Cimon**. But Demosthenes, on the other side (as Demetrius sayeth), was no man to trust to for wars, neither had he any power to refuse gifts and bribes. For, though he would never be corrupted by Philip king of Macedon, yet he was bribed with gold and silver that was brought from the cities of **Susa and Ecbatana**; and was very ready to praise and commend the deeds of their ancestors, but not to follow them.

Truly, yet was he the honestest man of all other orators in his time, excepting Phocion. And besides, he did ever speak more boldly and plainly to the people than any man else, and would openly contrary their minds, and sharply reprove the Athenians for their faults, as appeareth by his orations. Theopompus also writeth, that the people on a time would have had him to accuse a man, whom they would needs have condemned. But he refusing to do it, the people were offended, and did **mutiny** against him. Thereupon he rising up, said openly unto them:

> "O ye men of Athens, I will always counsel ye to
> that which I think best for the benefit of the
> commonwealth, although it be against your minds:
> but falsely to accuse one, to satisfy your minds,
> though you command me, I will not do it."

And his conduct in the case of **Antiphon** was perfectly **aristocratical**; whom, after he had been acquitted in the assembly, he took and brought before the **court of Areopagus**; and, setting at naught the displeasure of the people, convicted him there of having promised Philip to **burn the arsenal**; whereupon the man was condemned by that court, and suffered for it.

[omission while Plutarch rambles a bit]

Part Two

Now before the war with Macedon began, it was evident enough what course Demosthenes would steer in the commonwealth: for whatever was done by the Macedonian, he criticized and found fault with, and upon all occasions was stirring up the people of Athens, and inflaming them against him [Philip]. Therefore, in the court of Philip, no man was so much talked of, or of so great account as he; and when he came thither, **one of the ten ambassadors who were sent into Macedonia**, though all had audience given them, yet his speech was answered with most care and exactness. But in other respects, Philip entertained him not so honourably as the rest, neither did he show him the same kindness and civility with which he applied himself to the party of Aeschines and Philocrates. Wherefore when they did highly praise Philip, and said that he was a well-spoken prince, a **fair** man, and would drink freely and be pleasant in company: Demosthenes smiled at it, and turned all those things to the worst, saying that those qualities were nothing commendable nor meet for a king. For the first was a quality meet for a **pleader**, the second for a woman, and the third for a sponge.

But when things came at last to war because Philip of the one side could not live in peace, and the Athenians on the other side were still incensed and stirred up by Demosthenes' daily orations, the first action he put them upon was **the reducing of Euboea**, which, by the treachery of the **tyrants**, was brought under subjection to Philip. And on his proposition, the decree was voted, and they crossed over thither and chased the Macedonians out of the island.

After that also he (Demosthenes) caused them to send aid unto the Byzantines, and unto the Perinthians, with whom Philip made war. He (Demosthenes) persuaded the people to lay aside their enmity against these cities, to forget the offences committed by them in the Confederate War, and to send them such aid as eventually saved and secured them.

Not long after, he undertook an embassy through the states of Greece, which he solicited and so far incensed against Philip that, a few only excepted, **he brought them all into a general league**.

So that, besides the forces composed of the citizens themselves, there was an army consisting of fifteen thousand foot and two thousand horse, and the money to pay these **strangers** was levied and brought in with great cheerfulness. On which occasion it was, says Theophrastus, on the allies requesting that their contributions for the war might ascertained and stated, Crobylus the orator made use of the saying, "War can't be fed at so much a day."

Narration and Discussion

"His greatest foes, which were most against him, were driven to confess that they had to do with a famous man." Demosthenes was recognized as someone out of the ordinary, even by his enemies such as Philip of Macedon. According to this passage, what quality in particular made his speeches stand out?

After the visit to the Macedonian court, the Athenian ambassadors praised Philip for being well-spoken, physically attractive, and someone who would "drink freely." Demosthenes turned the compliments into insults and said those were not good qualities for a king. Do you agree?

How did Demosthenes use his own "well-spokenness" in the struggle against the Macedonians?

Creative narration #1: Write a letter or a journal entry by Demosthenes, describing his experience at Philip's court. (**Trivia:** according to Aeschines' account, Demosthenes collapsed from nervousness in the middle of a speech.)

Lesson Five

Introduction

In 340 B.C., Demosthenes convinced the Athenians to break the Peace of Philocrates by sending aid to Perinthus and Byzantium. They knew that, if they did so, they would probably end up fighting a battle with Philip; and in that case, they were going to need allies.

Demosthenes had a difficult task: to use his gifts of persuasion to bring the Thebans, the often-unfriendly neighbours of the Athenians, into an alliance against their common enemy. He offered two important words to the Thebans: honour and honesty. However; the day of Greek power had already ended, and even Demosthenes' eloquence could not change that.

Vocabulary

up in arms: prepared for war

in a league: alliance, team

pleasures: benefits, favours

vicinity: the closeness of their borders

success at Amphissa: also called the **Fourth Sacred War**

in a great consternation: greatly upset and confused

perplexity: uncertainty as to what action to take

firing their emulation: stirring up their ambition

in a sort of divine possession: enraptured by his words (more literally, as if they had been possessed by some supernatural force)

was up: was aroused

to put a period...to: to put an end to

Pythian priestess, Sibyl, oracle: These are all terms having to do with the Oracle at Delphi, a sacred place where prophecies were believed to come through a priestess. In this case, the people uncovered an old message that seemed to pertain to the current situation.

belie: contradict; betray

came to himself: calmed down, became serious (North says "waxed sober")

give Philip occupation: keep him busy and out of the way

People

Epaminondas: a famous Greek general of Thebes

the king: The monarchy of Persia was in flux at this time, as Artaxerxes III died in 338 B.C. and was replaced by several short-lived successors, before the last of them was killed by Alexander. It sounds, though, that Plutarch is speaking here about events before the **Battle of Chaeronea**, so that would still be Artaxerxes.

Historic Occasions

338 B.C.: Amphissa destroyed by Macedon; Athenians and Thebans became allies against Macedon

338 B.C.: Battle of Chaeronea, which the Greeks lost to the Macedonians (and in which Demades was taken prisoner)

On the Map

Amphissa (or Amfissa): a town in Phocis

Elateia: a city of Phthiotis

Sardis: a city which is now part of Turkey

Reading

Part One

Now all Greece was **up in arms**, attending what should happen. The Euboaeans, the Athenians, the Corinthians, the Megarians, the Leucadians, and the Corcyraeans, their people and their cities, were all joined together **in a league**. But the hardest task was yet behind, left for Demosthenes, to draw the Thebans into this confederacy with the rest. Their country bordered next upon Attica; they had great forces for the war; and at that time they were accounted the best soldiers of all Greece, but it was no easy matter to make them break with Philip, who but lately before had bound them unto him by many great **pleasures** which he had done to them, in the War of the Phocians: besides also that betwixt Athens and Thebes, by reason of **vicinity**, there fell out daily quarrels and debates, the which with every little thing were soon renewed.

But after Philip, being now grown high and puffed up with his good **success at Amphissa**, on a sudden surprised **Elateia** and possessed himself of **Phocis**, and the Athenians were **in a great consternation**, none dared venture to rise up to speak, no one knew what to say, all were at a loss, and the whole assembly in silence and **perplexity**. In this extremity of affairs Demosthenes was the only man who appeared, his counsel to them being alliance with the Thebans. And having in other ways encouraged the people, and as his manner was, raised their spirits up with hopes, he, with some others, was sent as ambassador to Thebes. Philip also for his part, sent ambassadors unto the Thebans, Amyntas and Clearchus, two Macedonians, and with them, Daochus, Thessalus, and Thrasydaeus, to answer and withstand the persuasions of the Athenian ambassadors.

Now, the Thebans, in their consultations, were well enough aware what suited best with their own interest; but everyone had before his eyes the terrors of war, and their losses in the Phocian troubles were still recent; but such as the force and power of the orator fanning up, as Theopompus says, their courage, and **firing their emulation**, that, casting away every thought of prudence, fear, or obligation, **in a sort of divine possession**, they chose the path of honour to which his words invited them.

This act of an orator was of so great force, that Philip forthwith sent ambassadors unto the Grecians, to entreat for peace, and all Greece **was up**, to see what would become of this stir. Thus, not only the captains of Athens obeyed Demosthenes, doing all that he commanded them; but the governors also of Thebes, and of all the country of Boeotia besides. And the assemblies also of the council of Thebes were as well governed by him, as the assemblies of Athens, being alike beloved both of the one and the other, and having a like authority to command both, and not undeservedly, as Theopompus sayeth, but indeed it was no more than was due to his merit.

Part Two

But there was, it would seem, some divinely ordered fortune, commissioned, in the revolution of things, **to put a period at this time to** the liberty of Greece, which opposed and thwarted all their actions, and by many signs foretold what should happen. Such were the sad predictions uttered by the **Pythian priestess**, and this old **oracle** cited out of the **Sibyl's** verses:—

> The battle on Thermodon that shall be

Safe at a distance I desire to see,

For, like an eagle, watching in the air,

Conquered shall weep, and conqueror perish there.

[Omission for length: argument over the identity of Thermodon]

But of Demosthenes, it is said that he had such great confidence in the Grecian forces, and was so excited by the sight of the courage and resolution of so many brave men ready to engage the enemy, that he would by no means endure they should give any need to oracles, or hearken to prophecies; but gave out that he suspected even the prophetess herself, as if she had been tampered with to speak in favour of Philip. The Thebans he put in mind of **Epaminondas**; the Athenians of Pericles, who always took their own measures and governed their actions by reason, looking upon things of this kind as mere pretexts for cowardice.

Part Three

Thus far, therefore, Demosthenes acquitted himself like a brave man. But in the fight [the **Battle of Chaeronia**], he did nothing honourable, nor was his performance answerable to his speeches. For he fled, deserting his place disgracefully, and throwing away his arms, not ashamed, as Pytheas observed, to **belie** the inscription written on his shield, in letters of gold, "With good fortune."

[Plutarch gives few details here about the battle, other than Demosthenes' less-than-memorable part in it. The result was that the armies of Athens and Thebes were destroyed, and the Greeks were now under the rule of Macedon.]

Part Four

In the meantime Philip, in the first moment of victory, was so transported with joy, that he grew extravagant. For after he had drunk well with his friends, he went into the place where the overthrow was given, and there in mockery began to sing the beginning of the decree which Demosthenes had preferred, (by the which, the Athenians accordingly proclaimed wars against him) rising and falling with his voice, and dancing it in measure with his foot:

Demosthenes, the son of Demosthenes,

did put forth this.

But when he **came to himself**, and had remembered himself what danger he had been in: then his hair stood bolt upright upon his head, considering the force and power of such an orator, that in a piece of a day had enforced him to hazard his realm and life at a battle.

Now Demosthenes' fame was so great that it was carried even to the court of Persia, and **the king** sent letters to his lieutenants and governors, that they should supply Demosthenes with money, and to pay every attention to him, as the only man of all the Grecians who was able to **give Philip occupation**, and find employment for his forces near home, in the troubles of Greece. (This afterwards came to the knowledge of Alexander, by certain letters of Demosthenes which he found at **Sardis**, and by other papers of the Persian officers, stating the large sums which had been given him.)

Narration and Discussion

Why was the king of Persia so interested in helping the Greek cause?

Why did Philip believe that the Battle of Chaeronea was influenced by the power of Demosthenes' words? Was he right?

Creative narration: Draw a newspaper cartoon for one of the events in this lesson. (One idea: a new shield for Demosthenes?)

Creative narration for older students: William Shakespeare used North's translation of Plutarch's *Lives* as source material for various plays, such as *Julius Caesar* and *Coriolanus*. Imagine that he had decided to write a play based on the *Life of Demosthenes*. Write/act out a scene based on this passage:

"In the meantime Philip, in the first moment of victory, was so transported with joy, that he grew extravagant."

Or on this one:

"But of Demosthenes… would by no means endure they should give any need to oracles, or hearken to prophecies; but gave out that he suspected even the prophetess herself, as if she had been tampered with to speak in favour of Philip."

Lesson Six

Introduction

What is luck? In the aftermath of the Battle of Chaeronea, Demosthenes wondered if his luck had run out…or if, even worse, his leadership was now unlucky for the Athenians.

Vocabulary

> **sorrow or grief:** that is, they were certainly sorrowful, but they did not seem to blame Demosthenes for the disaster

> **subscribe any:** put his name to any of them

> **to prevent the sinister luck and misfortune of his name:** because he believed that his own bad luck might be transferred to others

> **chaplet:** a wreath worn on the head

> **reproveth:** criticizes

> **clemency:** mercy

> **a base thing:** a dishonourable act

> **Fortune:** Plutarch refers to Fortune as a female deity, called *Fortuna* in Latin; the Greek equivalent was *Tyche*.

> **when they list:** when they feel like it

> **assuage:** comfort; lessen his grief

People

Pausanias: Pausanias of Orestis, a bodyguard of Philip who stabbed
him to death (the exact reasons are unclear)

Historic Occasions

336 B.C.: the assassination of Philip II, and the accession of Alexander
as king of Macedon

Reading

Part One

Now, the Grecians being thus overthrown by battle, the other orators,
adversaries unto Demosthenes in the commonwealth, began to set
upon him, and to prepare to accuse him. But the people did not only
clear him of all the accusations objected against him, but did continue
to honour him more than before, and to call him to assemblies, as one
that loved the honour and benefit of his country.

So that when the bones of their countrymen which were slain at the
Battle of Chaeronea were brought to be openly buried according to the
custom: the people gave him the honour to make the funeral oration
in praise of the dead. They made no show of **sorrow or grief** for the
loss they had received (as Theopompus writes in his exaggerated style);
but on the contrary, by the honour and respect paid to their counsellor,
they made it appear that they were no way dissatisfied with the counsels
he had given them.

Demosthenes then did make the funeral oration. But afterwards,
in all the decrees he preferred to the people, he would never **subscribe
any, to prevent the sinister luck and misfortune of his name**, but
did pass it under his friends' names one after another, until he grew
courageous again, shortly after that he understood of the death of
Philip, who was slain immediately after the victory he won at
Chaeronea. And it seemeth this was the meaning of the prophecy or
oracle in the two last verses:

Conquered shall weep, and conqueror perish there.

Part Two

Now Demosthenes, hearing of Philip's death before the news was openly known, thought he would put the people again into a good hope of better luck to come. Thereupon he went with a cheerful countenance into the assembly of the council, and told them there, that he had had a certain dream that promised great good fortune for Athens; and immediately after, the messengers arrived that brought certain news of King Philip's death. Thereupon the Athenians made sacrifices of joy to the gods for this happy news, and appointed a crown unto **Pausanias** that had slain him. Demosthenes also came abroad in a rich dress, with a **chaplet** on his head, though it were but the seventh day since the death of his daughter, as Aeschines reporteth: who **reproveth** him for it, and noteth him to be a man having little love or charity unto his own children. But indeed Aeschines himself deserveth more blame, to have such a tender, "womanish" heart as to believe that blubbering, weeping, and lamenting are signs of a gentle and charitable nature, condemning them that with patience and constancy do pass away such misfortunes.

For my own part, I cannot say that the behaviour of the Athenians on this occasion was wise or honourable, to crown themselves with garlands and to sacrifice to the gods for the death of a prince who, in the midst of his success and victories, when they were a conquered people, had used them with so much **clemency** and humanity. For besides provoking **Fortune**, it was **a base thing**, and unworthy in itself, to make him a citizen of Athens, and pay him honours while he lived, and yet as soon as he fell by another's hand, to set no bounds to their jollity, to insult over him dead, and to sing triumphant songs of victory, as if by their own valour they had vanquished him.

In contrary manner also, I praise and commend the constancy and courage of Demosthenes, that he, leaving the tears and lamentation of his home trouble unto women, did himself in the meantime that which he thought was for the benefit of the commonwealth: and in my opinion, I think he did therein like a man of courage, and worthy to be a governor of a commonwealth, never to stoop nor yield, but always to be found stable and constant, for the benefit of the commonwealth, rejecting all his troubles, cares, and affections, in respect of the service of his country, and to keep his honour much more carefully, than common players use to do, when they play the parts of kings and princes, whom we see neither weep nor laugh **when they list**, though they be on the stage, but when the matter of the play falleth out to give them just occasion. But omitting those reasons, if there be no reason (as indeed there is not) to leave and forsake a man in his sorrow and trouble, without giving him some words of comfort, and rather to devise some matter to **assuage** his sorrow, and to withdraw his mind from that, to think upon some pleasanter things: even as they should keep sore eyes from seeing bright and glaring colours, in offering them green and darker. And from whence can a man take greater comfort for his troubles and griefs at home, when the commonwealth doth well, than to join their private griefs with common joys, to the end, that the better may obscure and take away the worse?

But thus far I digressed from my history, enlarging this matter, because Aeschines, in his oration touching this matter, did move the people's hearts too much to "womanish" sorrow.

Narration and Discussion

Why were the Athenians grateful rather than resentful to Demosthenes?

Do you think Demosthenes was "unlucky?" Explain.

For further thought: Aeschines criticized Demosthenes for rejoicing with the Athenians, and not showing proper respect to his own daughter who had died. What would you say?

Creative narration: Retell the events of this lesson in any format you like (interview, newspaper headlines, drawing, drama).

Lesson Seven

Introduction

A new era had begun, with the accession of Alexander as king of Macedon. Alexander summoned Demosthenes, along with other "bright lights" of Athens: it was an invitation they couldn't refuse.

The last paragraph of this lesson describes an event that Plutarch assumes we already know about. In 336 B.C., an orator named Ctesiphon had proposed that Athens honour Demosthenes for his stand against Macedon, by presenting him with a golden crown. Ctesiphon was **indicted**, several years later, because his proposal had violated Athenian law. (This seems to have been as much an attack on Demosthenes as it was on Ctesiphon.) Demosthenes made a famous speech, "On the Crown," in his defense.

Vocabulary

resolved to send ambassadors to Alexander: As punishment for their rebellion, Alexander had demanded that all anti-Macedonian politicians in Athens be sent into exile. The embassy was intended to plead for mercy in this, but it apparently succeeded only because of Demades' actions.

gave up the embassy: left the mission, went home

mastiffs: dogs

corn masters: like travelling salespeople with samples

the persons whom Alexander had demanded: the ambassadors

put aside: North says "under foot"

vanquished: conquered

indictment: accusation, formal charges

archon: head of the city (North translates this "mayor")

suffrages: votes

People

Aristobulus of Cassandrea: a Greek historian, architect, engineer; a friend of Alexander the Great

Agis the Spartan: King Agis III (not the Agis IV of *Agis and Cleomenes*)

Ctesiphon: see notes above. Rough pronunciation guide: "**Tess**-a-fun."

Aeschines: Aeschines was prosecuting Ctesiphon (and lost the case).

Historic Occasions

335 B.C.: Demosthenes started a rumour that Alexander had been killed in battle, which incited a rebellion by the Athenians and the Thebans. Alexander then destroyed Thebes and captured its people.

334 B.C.: Alexander invaded the Persian Empire

333 B.C.: With support from the Persian king, Agis III of Sparta recovered the island of Crete from the Macedonians

331 B.C.: Agis died at the Battle of Megalopolis

330 B.C.: Trial of Ctesiphon

330 B.C.: Alexander burned Persepolis (the Persian capital city)

On the Map

Boeotia: a region of central Greece

Mount Cithaeron: a mountain range which formed the boundary between **Boeotia** and **Attica** (the region of Athens)

Rhodes: a large island, northeast of Crete and southeast of Athens

Ionia: a Greek colony, located in present-day Turkey

Reading

The cities of Greece, being again stirred up by Demosthenes, made a new league again together. The Thebans, whom he had provided with arms, set upon the (Macedonian) garrison, and slew many of them; the Athenians made preparations to join their forces with them; Demosthenes ruled supreme in the popular assembly, and wrote letters to the Persian officers who commanded under the king in Asia, inciting them to make war upon the Macedonian, calling him (Alexander) "child" and "simpleton."

But as soon as Alexander had settled matters in his own country, and came in person with his army into **Boeotia**, down fell the courage of the Athenians, and Demosthenes was hushed. At length, the poor Thebans being left unto themselves, forsaken of every man, they were compelled themselves alone to bear the brunt of this war, and so came their city to utter ruin and destruction.

After which, the people of Athens, all in distress and great perplexity, **resolved to send ambassadors to Alexander**, and amongst others, made choice of Demosthenes for one; but his heart failing him for fear of the king's anger, he returned back from **Mount Cithaeron**, and **gave up the embassy**. But Alexander sent to Athens requiring ten of their orators to be delivered up to him, as Idomeneus and Duris have reported, but as the most and best historians say, he demanded these eight only: Demosthenes, Polyeuctus, Ephialtes, Lycurgus, Myrocles, Damon, Callisthenes, and Charidemus.

At which time, they write that Demosthenes told the people of Athens the fable of the sheep and wolves, how that the wolves came on a time, and willed the sheep, if they would have peace with them, to deliver them their **mastiffs** that kept them. And so he compared himself, and his companions that travelled for the benefit of the country, unto the dogs that keep the flocks of sheep, and calling Alexander the wolf. He further told them, "As we see **corn-masters** sell their whole stock by a few grains of wheat which they carry about with them in a dish, as a sample of the rest, so you by delivering up us, who are but a few, do at the same time unawares surrender up yourselves all together with us." (So we find it related in the history of **Aristobulus of Cassandrea**.)

The Athenians were deliberating, and at a loss what to do, when Demades, having agreed with **the persons whom Alexander had demanded**, for five talents, undertook to go as an ambassador, and to intercede with the king for them; either because he trusted in the love the king did bear him, or else for that he thought he hoped he should find him pacified, as a lion glutted with the blood of beasts which he had slain. Howsoever it happened, he persuaded the people to send him unto him, and so handled Alexander, that he got their pardon, and did reconcile him with the city of Athens.

So he (Demades) and his friends, when Alexander went away, were great men, and Demosthenes was quite **put aside**. Yet when **Agis the Spartan** made his insurrection, he also for a short time attempted a movement in his favour; but he soon shrunk back again, as the Athenians would not take any part in it, and, Agis being slain, the Lacedaemonians were **vanquished**.

During this time it was that the **indictment** against **Ctesiphon, concerning the crown**, was brought to trial. The action was commenced a little before the Battle of Chaeronea, when Chaerondus was **archon**, but it was not proceeded with till about ten years after, Aristophon being then archon. Never was any public cause more celebrated than this, alike for the fame of the orators, and for the generous courage of the judges, who, though at the time the accusers of Demosthenes were in the height of power, and supported by all the favour of the Macedonians, yet would not give judgment against him, but acquitted him so honourably, that **Aeschines** did not obtain the fifth part of their **suffrages** on his side; so that, immediately after, he left the city, and spent the rest of his life in teaching rhetoric about the island of **Rhodes**, and upon the continent in **Ionia**.

Narration and Discussion

Did things get better or worse for Greece after the death of Philip? What surprising turn of events took place with Demades?

Was it Demosthenes' fault that it was suggested he be given a crown?

Creative narration #1: Retell the fable of the Wolves and the Sheep.

Creative narration #2: Taking the part of a television reporter or interviewer, tell about the events of the Ctesiphon trial.

Lesson Eight

Introduction

In this lesson we are introduced to Harpalus, a former friend of King Alexander, and (we are told right away) a scoundrel who knew how to exploit people's greed. But could he outsmart Demosthenes?

Vocabulary

terrible: frightening, terrifying

to their disposal: to use as they chose

an armed garrison: a troop of soldiers

citadel: fortress

swathed about…: muffled up as if he had a sore throat

wits: jokers

"silver quinsy": We might say today, "a bit of silver-itis."

cup-bearer: At feasts, a cup of wine was passed from person to person, and the one who held the cup was permitted (or expected) to entertain the others by speaking or singing.

pilfered: stolen, embezzled

inquisition: close examination, investigation

fortitude: strength and courage in a time of trouble

Acropolis: the hill overlooking Athens, site of the temple of **Athena**

Lady Minerva: the Greek goddess **Athena**, who, besides being the patron goddess of Athens, also represented wisdom and justice

intractable: untamable, hard to control

People

Harpalus: an aristocrat of Macedon, and boyhood friend of Alexander

Historic Occasions

326 B.C.: Alexander invaded India

324 B.C.: Harpalus arrived in Athens

On the Map

Aegina: an island in the **Saronic Gulf**

Troezen: a town in the northeastern **Peloponnese**

Reading

Part One

It was not long after that **Harpalus** fled from Alexander, and came to Athens out of Asia; knowing himself guilty of many misdeeds into which his love of luxury had led him, and fearing the king, who was now grown **terrible** even to his best friends. Yet this man had no sooner addressed himself to the people, and delivered up his goods, his ships, and himself **to their disposal**, but the other orators of the town had their eyes quickly fixed upon his money, and came in to his assistance, and did counsel the people to receive and protect a poor suitor that came to them for aid.

But Demosthenes gave counsel to the contrary, and bade them rather drive Harpalus out of the city, and take heed they brought not wars upon their backs for a matter that not only was not necessary, but furthermore merely unjust. But within a few days after, inventory being taken of all Harpalus' goods, he perceiving that Demosthenes took great pleasure to see a cup of the king's, and considered very curiously the fashion and workmanship upon it: he gave it him in his hand, to judge what it weighed. Demosthenes, being amazed to feel how heavy it was, asked him what weight it came *to*. "To you," said Harpalus, smiling, "it shall come *with* twenty talents." And presently after, when night drew on, he sent him the cup with so many talents.

This Harpalus was a very wise man, and found straight by Demosthenes' countenance that he loved money; and could presently judge his nature, by seeing his pleasant countenance, and his eyes still upon the cup. For Demosthenes could not resist the temptation, but admitting the present, like **an armed garrison**, into the **citadel** of his house, he surrendered himself up to the interest of Harpalus.

The next morning, Demosthenes went into the assembly of the people, having his neck **swathed about with wool and rollers**. So when they called him by his name to step up into the pulpit, to speak to the people as he had done before: he made a sign with his head, that he had an impediment in his voice, and that he could not speak. But the **wits**, turning the matter to ridicule, said that certainly the orator had been seized that night with no other than a **"silver quinsy."** Afterwards when the people understood that he was corrupted, Demosthenes going about to excuse himself, they would not abide to hear him: but made a noise and exclamation against him; and one man stood up and cried out, "What, ye men of Athens, will you not hear the **cup-bearer?**"

The people thereupon did immediately banish Harpalus, and fearing lest King Alexander would require an account of the gold and silver, which the orators had robbed and **pilfered** away among them: they made very diligent search and inquiry in every man's house, excepting Callicles' house, the son of Arrenidas, whose house they would have searched by no means, because he was but newly married, and had his new spouse in his house, as Theopompus writeth.

Part Two

Demosthenes resisted this **inquisition**, and proposed a decree to refer the business to the court of the Areopagus, and to punish those whom that court should find guilty. Howbeit he was one of the first whom the court condemned in the sum of fifty talents, and for lack of payment, they put him in prison: where he could not endure long, both for the shame of the matter for which he was condemned, as also for his sickly body. So he made his escape, by the carelessness of some and by the contrivance of others of the citizens.

We are told, at least, that he had not fled far from the city when, finding that he was pursued by some of those who had been his adversaries, he endeavoured to hide himself. But when they called him by his name, and coming up nearer to him, desired he would accept from them some money which they had brought from home as a provision for his journey, and to that purpose only had followed him; when they entreated him to take courage, and to bear up against his misfortune, he burst out into much greater lamentation, saying, "Why, would you not have me be sorry for my misfortune, that compelleth me to forsake the city where indeed I have so courteous enemies, that it is hard for me to find anywhere so good friends?"

He did not show much **fortitude** in his banishment, spending his time for the most part in **Aegina** and **Troezen**, and with tears in his eyes, looking towards the country of Attica. And there remain upon record some sayings of his, little resembling those sentiments of generosity and bravery which he used to express when he had the management of the commonwealth. For, as he was departing out of the city, it is reported, he lifted up his hands towards the **Acropolis**, and said, "O **Lady Minerva**, how is it that thou takest delight in three such fierce **intractable** beasts: the owl, the dragon [*Dryden: the snake*], and the people?"

Besides, he persuaded the young men that came to see him, and that were with him, never to meddle in matters of state, assuring them, that if they had offered him two ways at the first, the one to go into the assembly of the people, to make orations in the pulpit, and the other to be put to death presently, and that he had known as he did then, the troubles a man is compelled to suffer that meddleth with the affairs of the state, the fear, the envy, the accusations, and troubles in the same: he would rather have chosen the way to have suffered death.

Narration and Discussion

Were you surprised by Demosthenes' actions in this lesson?

When Demosthenes was banished, what was his somewhat bitter advice to young people? Do you agree?

Creative narration: There are some good opportunities here for dramatic narration (see also the Shakespeare activity in **Lesson Five**).

For older students: Those who have read Robert Bolt's play *A Man for All Seasons* may want to compare this passage with the story of a cup that caused Sir Thomas More similar trouble.

Lesson Nine

Introduction

The world turned upside down again with the sudden death of Alexander. Cities chose unexpected allies and made enemies of former friends; people did the same. Certain orators fleeing Athens made it their business to preach against Greek alliances; but Demosthenes, even in banishment, made an unexpectedly loyal, and costly, stand for his city.

Vocabulary

straitly besieged: shut in, imprisoned

fled from Athens: Pytheas, at least, was more likely banished.

rencounter: chance meeting

railing: loud argument, sharp words

asses' milk: donkeys' milk, long believed to have healing properties

pecuniary fine: the amount of money he had been charged

Jupiter Soter: the Greek god Zeus

Metageitnion, Boedromion, Pyanepsion: three successive months

privily: secretly

apprehend: arrest

temple of Ajax: The mythical hero Ajax was worshipped by the Athenians.

light vessels: small boats

People

Leosthenes: commander of the Greek forces against Macedon

48

Antipater: Macedonian general and statesman

Callimedon: An orator who headed the pro-Macedonian party in Athens. He was nicknamed "The Crab" or, more literally, "The Spiny Lobster," not because of his appearance or disposition, but because he liked to eat them.

Phylarchus: a Greek historian whose works are now lost

Demetrius of Magnesia: a biographer

Alcibiades: see **Lesson One**

Craterus: Macedonian general, allied with Antipater

Archias: a former actor, now a soldier in Antipater's army, who acted as a bounty-hunter

Historic Occasions

323 B.C.: the death of Alexander (of causes which are still disputed)

323-322 B.C.: Lamian War between Athens/the Aetolian League against Macedonia/Boeotia

322 B.C.: Battle of Crannon (the decisive battle of the Lamian War)

On the Map

Munichia (or Munychia): a steep hill in **Piraeus**, the town containing the port used by Athens

Cleonae: a city in the Peloponnese

Calauria (Kalaureia): an island close to the coast of **Troezen**

Reading

Part One

But now happened the death of Alexander, while Demosthenes was in this banishment which we have been speaking of. And the Grecians were once again up in arms, encouraged by the brave attempts of **Leosthenes**, who, being a man of great valour, had shut up **Antipater** in the city of Lamia, and there kept him **straitly besieged**. Pytheas (who had prosecuted Demosthenes), and **Callimedon**, called the Crab, both **fled from Athens**, and taking sides with Antipater [that is, to promote the Macedonian cause], went about with his friends and ambassadors to keep the other Grecians from revolting and taking part with the Athenians. But, on the other side, Demosthenes, associating himself with the ambassadors that came from Athens, used his utmost endeavours and gave them his best assistance in persuading the cities to fall unanimously upon the Macedonians, and to drive them out of Greece. **Phylarchus** says that in Arcadia there happened a **rencounter** between Pytheas and Demosthenes, which came at last to downright **railing**, while the one pleaded for the Macedonians, and the other for the Grecians. Pytheas, having spoken before him, had said: "Like as we presume always that there is some sickness in the house whither we do see **asses' milk** brought: so must that town of necessity be sick, wherein the ambassadors of Athens do enter." Demosthenes answered him again, turning his comparison against him: that indeed they brought asses' milk, where there was need to recover health: and even so, the ambassadors of Athens were sent to heal and cure them that were sick.

The people at Athens understanding what Demosthenes had done, they so rejoiced at it, that presently they gave order in the field that his banishment should be revoked. (The decree was brought in by Daemon the Paenian, cousin to Demosthenes.)

He landed at the port of Piraeus, where he was met and joyfully received by all the citizens, not so much as an archon or a priest staying behind. And **Demetrius of Magnesia** says that he lifted up his hands towards heaven, and blessed this day of his happy return, as far more honourable than that of **Alcibiades**; since he was recalled by his countrymen, not through any force or constraint put upon them, but by their own goodwill and free inclinations. There remained only his **pecuniary fine**, which, according to law, could not be remitted by the people. But they found out a way to elude the law. It was a custom with them to allow a certain quantity of silver to those who were to furnish and adorn the altar for the sacrifice of **Jupiter Soter**. This office, for that turn, they bestowed on Demosthenes, and for the performance of it ordered him fifty talents, the very sum in which he was condemned.

Part Two

Yet it was no long time that he enjoyed his country after his return, the attempts of the Greeks being soon all utterly defeated. For the **Battle of Crannon** happened in **Metageitnion**; in **Boedromion** the garrison entered into **Munychia**; and in the **Pyanepsion** following died Demosthenes, after this manner.

When news came to Athens that Antipater and **Craterus** were coming thither with a great army, Demosthenes and his friends took their opportunity to escape **privily** out of the city; but sentence of death was, upon the motion of Demades, passed upon them by the people. They dispersed themselves, flying some to one place, some to another; and Antipater sent about his soldiers into all quarters to **apprehend** them. **Archias** was their captain, and was thence called "the Exile-hunter." (He was a Thurian born, and is reported to have been an actor of tragedies; and they say that Polus, of Aegina, the best actor of his time, was his scholar; but Hermippus reckons Archias among the disciples of Lacritus, the orator, and Demetrius says he spent some time with Anaximenes.)

Now, this Archias having found the orator Hyperides in the city of Aegina, and Aristonicus Marathonian, and Himeraeus the brother of Demetrius of Phalerum, which had taken sanctuary in the **temple of Ajax**: he took them out of the temple by force, and sent them unto Antipater, who was at that time in **Cleonae**, where he did put them all to death: and some say that he did cut off Hyperides' tongue. Furthermore, hearing that Demosthenes had taken sanctuary in the isle of **Calauria**, he took some **light vessels**, and a certain number of Thracian soldiers, and being come thither, he sought to persuade Demosthenes to be contented to go with him unto Antipater, promising him that he should have no hurt.

Narration and Discussion

Describe Demosthenes' homecoming. What happened to his fine?

Should he have been made to pay it himself? (See Proverbs 17:26)

How did things deteriorate afterwards?

Creative narration #1: See the Shakespeare activity in **Lesson Five**.

Creative narration #2: You are the editor and chief reporter for a monthly news report called the *Athens Advocate*. Show the front page and headlines for the Metagitnion, Boedromion, or Pyanepsion issue.

Lesson Ten and Examination Questions

Introduction

Demosthenes' death was tragic; but the memory of his life inspired memorials and even, if one can believe it, miracles.

Vocabulary

contending with Archias: in a contest with him for a drama prize

furniture and provision for the stage: theatrical equipment

forbear only a little: wait just a few minutes; be patient

he cast his gown over his head, and laid him down: Dryden says "he bowed down his head and covered it."

play Creon's part: In the play *Antigone*, King Creon forbids the proper burial of Polynices.

Neptune: the god Poseidon

gave up the ghost: died

a piece of gold he had swallowed down: Dryden also says "gold which he swallowed." The exact meaning is not clear.

preservative: This word makes it sound as if Demosthenes was carrying a drug "for medicinal purposes"; but other translators have used the word "safeguard," implying that it was intended for a purpose such as he used it here, rather than a means to "preserve" his health.

running abroad in every man's mouth: being widely discussed

epigrams: verses (in this context); inscriptions

People

Archias: see previous lesson

Perdiccas: North includes a footnote that, in the *Life of Phocion*, Plutarch says Antigonus instead of Perdiccas. In any case, it was one of the rivals of Antipater.

Cassander: the son of Antipater

Historic Occasions

322 B.C.: the death of Demosthenes

Reading

Part One

Demosthenes had a strange dream the night before, and thought that he had played a tragedy **contending with Archias**, and that he handled himself so well, that all the lookers-on at the theater did commend him, and gave him the honour to be the best player; yet for want of better **furniture and provision for the stage**, he lost the day.

The next morning when Archias came to speak with him, Demosthenes used gentle words unto him, thinking thereby to win him by fair means to leave the sanctuary: Demosthenes, looking him full in the face, sitting still where he was, without removing, said unto him, "Archias, thou didst never persuade me when thou played a play, neither shalt thou now persuade me, though thou promise me."

Then Archias began to be angry with him, and to threaten him.

"Now," said Demosthenes, "you speak like the genuine Macedonian oracle; before you were but acting a part. Therefore **forbear only a little**, while I write a word or two home to my family."

After he had said so, he went into the temple as though he would have dispatched some letters, and did put the end of the quill in his mouth which he wrote withal, and bit it as his manner was when he did use to write anything, and held the end of the quill in his mouth a pretty while together: then **he cast his gown over his head, and laid him down**. Archias' soldiers seeing that, being at the door of the temple, laughing him to scorn (thinking he had done so for that he was afraid to die) called him "coward" and "beast." Archias also coming to him, prayed him to rise, and began to use the former persuasions to him, promising him that he would make Antipater his friend.

Then Demosthenes feeling the poison work, cast open his gown, and boldly looking Archias in the face, said unto him: "Now when thou wilt, **play Creon's part**, and throw my body to the dogs, without further grave or burial. For my part, O god **Neptune**, I do go out of thy temple being yet alive, because I will not profane it with my death: but Antipater, and the Macedonians, have not spared to defile thy sanctuary with blood, and cruel murder." After he had thus spoken and desired to be held up, because already he began to tremble and stagger, as he was going forward, and passing by the altar, he fell down, and, with a groan, **gave up the ghost**.

Part Two

Now touching the poison, Ariston reporteth that he sucked and drew it up into his mouth out of his quill, as we have said before. But one Pappus (from whom Hermippus has taken his history) writeth that when he was laid on the ground before the altar, they found the beginning of a letter which said: "Demosthenes unto Antipater," but no more. And that when his sudden death was much wondered at, the Thracian soldiers that were at the temple door reported that they saw him pluck the poison which he put into his mouth out of a little cloth he had, thinking to them that it had been **a piece of gold he had swallowed down**. Howbeit a maid of the house that served Demosthenes, being examined by Archias about it, told him that he had carried it about him a long time, for a **preservative** for him.

54

Eratosthenes writeth, that he kept this poison in a little box of gold made hollow within, the which he wore as a bracelet about his arm.

There are many writers also that do report his death diversely, but to recite them all it were in vain; yet I must not omit what is said by Demochares, the relation of Demosthenes, who is of opinion it was not by the help of poison that he met with so sudden and so easy a death, but that by the singular favour and providence of the gods he was thus rescued from the cruelty of the Macedonians. He died on the sixteenth of Pyanepsion, the most sad and solemn day of the Thesmophoria, which the women observe by fasting in the temple of the goddess.

Shortly after, the Athenians, to honour him as he deserved, did cast his image in brass, and made a law besides, that the oldest man of his house should forever be kept within the palace, at the charge of the commonwealth: and engraved these verses also upon the base of his image:

> Hadst thou, Demosthenes, had strength according
> to thy heart.

> The Macedons should not have wrought the Greeks
> such woe and smart. *(North's translation; see
> others under **Narration and Discussion**)*

But it is simply ridiculous to say, as some have related, that Demosthenes made these verses himself in Calauria, as he was about to take the poison.

Part Three

A little before I [*Dryden: he*] went to Athens, the following incident was said to have happened. A certain soldier being sent for to come unto his captain, did put such pieces of gold as he had into the hands of Demosthenes' statue, which had both his hands joined together: and there grew hard by it a great plane tree, divers leaves whereof either blown oft by wind by chance, or else put there of purpose by the soldier, covered so this gold, that it was there a long time, and no man found it: until such time as the soldier came again, and found it as he left it. Hereupon this matter **running abroad in every man's mouth**, there were divers wise men that took occasion of this subject, to make

epigrams in the praise of Demosthenes, as one who in his life was never corrupted.

Furthermore, Demades did not long enjoy the honour he thought he had newly gotten. For the justice of the gods, revenger of the death of Demosthenes, brought him into Macedon, to receive just punishment by death, of those whom he dishonestly flattered: being before grown hateful to them, and afterwards committed a fault whereby he could not escape. For there were letters of his taken, by the which he did persuade and pray **Perdiccas** to make himself king of Macedon, and to deliver Greece from bondage, saying that it hung but by a thread, and yet it was half rotten; meaning thereby, Antipater. Dinarchus the Corinthian accused him, that he wrote these letters: the which so grievously offended **Cassander**, that first he slew Demades' son Demeas, and then commanded that they should afterwards kill Demades, making him feel then by those miseries (which are the cruelest that can happen unto man) that traitors betraying their own country do first of all betray themselves. Demosthenes had often forewarned him of his end, but he would never believe him.

Thus, my friend Sosius, you have what we can deliver you, by reading, or report, touching Demosthenes' life and doings.

Narration and Discussion

Read the verses that were engraved upon the base of Demosthenes' statue. Here is an alternative translation (Langhorne's):

> "Divine in speech, in judgment, too, divine,
>
> Had valour's wreath, Demosthenes, been thine,
>
> Fair Greece had still her freedom's ensign borne."

And here is Dryden's version:

> "Had you for Greece been strong, as wise you were,
>
> The Macedonian had not conquered her."

Can you explain what is meant?

For older students: How might being a public speaker be considered a dangerous occupation? Can you think of modern examples?

Creative narration #1: See the Shakespeare activity in **Lesson Five**. (Write or act out any part of this lesson in a way that Shakespeare might have done.)

Creative narration #2 (for older students): Write an "epigram" for Demosthenes. Or create a "new translation" of the inscription above.

Examination Questions

For Younger Students

1. Give some account of how Demosthenes went to hear an orator who "bore the bell of eloquence," and how he then trained himself to become an orator.

For Older Students

1. "He won him marvellous fame for his great eloquence and plain manner of speech." By what means did Demosthenes attain this distinction?

2. (High School) Comment upon, with illustrations from his life, the celebrated inscription on the pedestal of Demosthenes' statue,—

"Had you for Greece been strong, as wise you were,

The Macedonian had not conquered her." (Dryden)

or

"Hadst thou, Demosthenes, had strength according
to thy heart.

 The Macedons should not have wrought the Greeks such
woe and smart." (North)

Comparison of Demosthenes and Cicero

This is as much as we could gather by our knowledge touching the notable acts and deeds worthy of memory, written of Cicero and Demosthenes. Furthermore, leaving the comparison aside of the difference of their eloquence in their orations: methinks I may say thus much of them. That Demosthenes did wholly employ all his wit and learning (natural or artificial) unto the art of rhetoric, and that in force, and virtue of eloquence, he did excel all the orators in his time: and for gravity and magnificent style, all those also that only write for shew or ostentation: and for sharpness and art, all the sophisters and masters of rhetoric. And that Cicero was a man generally learned in all sciences, and that had studied divers books, as appeareth plainly by the sundry books of philosophy of his own making, written after the manner of the Academic philosophers.

Furthermore, they may see in his orations he wrote in certain causes to serve him when he pleaded: that he sought occasions in his by-talk to shew men that he was excellently well learned. Furthermore, by their phrases a man may discern some spark of their manners and conditions. For Demosthenes' phrase hath no manner of fineness, jests, nor grace in it, but is altogether grave and harsh, and smelleth not of the lamp, as Pytheas said when he mocked him: but sheweth a great drinker of water, extreme pains, and therewith also a sharp and sour nature. But Cicero oftentimes fell from pleasant taunts, unto plain scurrility: and turning all his pleadings of matters of importance, to sport and laughter, having a grace in it, many times he did forget the comeliness that became a man of his calling. As in his oration for Caelius, where he sayeth, "It is no marvel if in so great abundance of wealth and fineness he give himself a little to take his pleasure: and that it was a folly not to use pleasures lawful, and tolerable, sith the famousest philosophers that ever were, did place the chief felicity of man, to be in pleasure." And it is reported also, that Marcus Cato having accused Muraena, Cicero being consul, defended his cause, and in his oration pleasantly girded all the sect of the Stoic philosophers for Cato's sake, for the strange opinions they hold, which they call paradoxes: insomuch as he made all the people and judges also fall a-laughing a-good. And Cato himself also smiling a little, said unto them that sat by him: "What a laughing and mocking consul have we, my lords?" But letting that pass, it seemeth that Cicero was of a pleasant and merry nature; for his face shewed ever great life and mirth in it. Whereas in Demosthenes' countenance on the other side, they might discern a marvelous diligence and care, and a pensive man, never weary with pain: insomuch that his enemies (as he reporteth himself) called him a perverse and froward man.

Furthermore, in their writings is discerned, that the one speaketh modestly in his own praise, so as no man can justly be offended with him: and yet not always, but when necessity enforceth him for some matter of great importance, but otherwise very discreet and modest to speak of himself. Cicero in contrary manner, using too often repetition of one self thing in all his orations, shewed an extreme ambition of glory, when incessantly he cried out: "Let spear and shield give place to gown / And give the tongue the laurel crown."

Yea, furthermore, he did not only praise his own acts and deeds, but the orations also which he had written or pleaded: as if he should have contended against Isocrates, or Anaximenes, a master that taught rhetoric, and not to go about to reform the people of Rome: "Which were both fierce and stout in arms / And fit to work their enemies harms." For, as it is requisite for a governor of a commonwealth to seek authority by his eloquence: so, to covet the praise of his own glorious tongue, or as it were to beg it, that sheweth a base mind. And therefore in this point we must confess that Demosthenes is far graver, and of a nobler mind: who declared himself, that all his eloquence came only but by practise, the which also required the favour of his auditory: and further, he thought them fools and mad men (as indeed they be no less) that therefore would make any boast of themselves. In this they were both alike, that both of them had great credit and authority in their orations to the people, and for their orations obtaining that they would propound: insomuch as captains, and they that had armies in their hands, stood in need of their eloquence. As Chares, Diopithes, and Leosthenes, they all were holpen of Demosthenes: and Pompey, and Octavius Caesar the young man, of Cicero: as Caesar himself confesseth in his Commentaries he wrote unto Agrippa, and Maecenas. But nothing sheweth a man's nature and condition more, (as it is reported, and so is it true) than when one is in authority: for that bewrayeth his humor, and the affections of his mind, and layeth open also all his secret vices in him. Demosthenes could never deliver any such proof of himself, because he never bare any office, nor was called forward. For he was not general of the army, which he himself had prepared against King Philip. Cicero on the other side being sent Treasurer into Sicily, and proconsul into Cilicia and Cappadocia, in such time as covetousness reigned most (insomuch that the captains and governors whom they sent to govern their provinces, thinking it villainy and dastardliness to rob, did violently take things by force, at what time also to take bribes was reckoned no shame, but to handle it discreetly, he was the better thought of, and beloved for it) he shewed plainly that he regarded not money, and gave forth many proofs of his courtesy and goodness.

Furthermore, Cicero being created consul by name, but dictator indeed, having absolute power and authority over all things to suppress the rebellion and conspirators of Catiline: he proved Plato's prophecy true, which was: that the cities are safe from danger, when the chief magistrates and governors (by some good divine fortune) do govern with wisdom and justice. Demosthenes was reproved for his corruption, and selling of his eloquence: because secretly he wrote one oration for Phormio, and another in the selfsame matter for Apollodorus, they being both adversaries. Further, he was defamed also for receiving money of the king of Persia, and therewithal condemned for the money which he had taken of Harpalus. And though some (peradventure) would object, that the reporters thereof (which are many) do lie: yet they can not possibly deny this, that Demosthenes had no power to refrain from looking of the presents which divers kings did offer him, praying him to accept them in good part for their sakes: neither was that the part of a man that did take usury by traffic on the sea, the extremest yet of all other. In contrary manner (as we have said before) it is certain that Cicero being treasurer, refused the gifts which the Sicilians offered him, there: and the presents also which the king of the Cappadocians offered him whilst he was proconsul in Cilicia, and those especially which his friends pressed upon him to take of them, being a great sum of money, when he went as a banished man out of Rome.

Furthermore, the banishment of the one was infamous to him, because by judgement he was banished as a thief. The banishment of the other was for as honourable an act as ever he did, being banished for ridding his country of wicked men. And therefore of Demosthenes, there was no speech after he was gone: but for Cicero, all the Senate changed their apparel into black, and determined that they would pass no decree by their authority, before Cicero's banishment was revoked by the people. Indeed Cicero idly passed his time of banishment, and did nothing all the while he was in Macedon: and one of the chiefest acts that Demosthenes did, in all the time that he dealt in the affairs of the commonwealth, was in his banishment. For he went unto every city, and did assist the ambassadors of the Grecians, and refused the ambassadors of the Macedonians. In the which he shewed himself a better citizen, than either Themistocles, or Alcibiades, in their like fortune and exile. So when he was called home, and returned, he fell again to his old trade which he practised before, and was ever against Antipater, and the Macedonians. Where Laelius in open Senate sharply took up Cicero, for that he sat still and said nothing, when that Octavius Caesar the young man made petition against the law, that he might sue for the consulship, and being so young, that he had never a hair on his face. And Brutus self also doth greatly reprove Cicero in his letters, for that he had maintained and nourished a more grievous and greater tyranny, than that which they had put down.

And last of all, me thinketh the death of Cicero most pitiful, to see an old man carried up and down, (with tender love of his servants) seeking all the ways that might be to flee death, which did not long prevent his natural course : and in the end, old as he was, to see his head so pitifully cut off. Whereas Demosthenes, though he yielded a little, entreating him that came to take him: yet for that he had prepared the poison long before, that he had kept it long, and also used it as he did, he cannot but be marvellously commended for it. For if the god Neptune denied him the benefit of his sanctuary, he betook him to a greater, and that was death: whereby he saved himself out of the soldiers' hands of the tyrant [Dryden: freeing himself from arms and soldiers], and also scorned the bloody cruelty of Antipater.

Marcus Tullius Cicero

(106 B.C.-43 B.C.)

Who was Cicero?

Cicero was a philosopher, historian, politician, and orator, who lived a long life (though not so long as he could have) during the final years of the Roman Republic. He had an enormous impact on language, writing, and philosophy, not only in his own world, but on Western civilization for centuries to come. When the Latin language didn't contain the words he needed, he created them. His prose style was admired above that of all other writers; and no-one (until this past century) was considered well-educated who had not studied Cicero's speeches and histories.

Strangely enough, there seems to be no P.N.E.U programme which included Plutarch's *Life of Cicero*, and we can only guess at possible reasons. One might be that there are several "necessary omissions," not so much about Cicero but about other people in the story. Another might be that there is some overlap with the *Lives* that the P.N.E.U. did cover often, such as *Julius Caesar*, though Cicero's own story is just as interesting and important.

Plutarch's focus, as always, is on character; but we also need to see Cicero against the background of his own time and place, and also understand how his life was affected by the actions of others. If Catiline had never attempted to overthrow the Republic, Cicero would not have had to make the hard and quick decision (like Publicola, centuries before) to execute two of the conspirators. If Clodius had not attempted to infiltrate "ladies' night" at Caesar's house (a perfect example, by the way, of acting Willfully but not with Will); and if Cicero's wife had not held a grudge against Clodius; then Cicero would not have had to deny Clodius's claim that he was out of town at the time, Caesar's marriage might have been saved, and Cicero would not have gained yet another bitter enemy and then been exiled. As they say, no good deed goes unpunished.

And finally there was the rise to power of Julius Caesar, and his assassination. Cicero was not one of Caesar's killers, but because of that event, and the speeches he made about it, he became an enemy of Mark Antony. Which, in those years, was not a good thing to be at all.

Cicero's Name (and Pronunciation)

How do you pronounce **Cicero**? In Latin, using classical pronunciation, it would be *Ki-ke-ro*. In English, it's acceptable to use soft C's: *Si-se-ro*. Cicero is sometimes referred to in English as "Tully," because of his second name, "Tullius."

Where did Cicero come from? Who were his relatives? Was he married?

Cicero was born in Arpi, about 60 miles (100 km) from the city of Rome. Some descriptions of him have taken that fact to imply that he was a bit of an outsider, so that he felt he had to strive both to succeed and to prove his "Roman-ness." In any case, although his family lived outside of the city, they were wealthy and of the quite-acceptable Equestrian social class. Both Cicero and his brother were sent to study with good teachers in Rome, and, later, Greece.

He married his first wife, **Terentia**, when he was 27 years old (she was about eight years younger), and they had two children, **Tullia** and **Cicero Minor** (or Junior). From Plutarch's descriptions, Terentia sounds somewhat domineering and unfriendly; but other mentions of her sound more positive; and in a letter Cicero wrote, he praised her courage and fortitude during a difficult time. Eventually, certain issues, such as a disagreement over their daughter's marriage, led to a divorce.

When a Roman couple divorced, the bride's dowry had to be repaid; and Terentia's dowry was a large one (it included tenement apartments and woodlands). This may be why Cicero soon married another wealthy woman named **Pubilia**; and, in fact, he insisted that he *had* married her for money, as that was less shameful (in his social circles) than appearing to be a foolish old man (he was sixty) in love with a young girl. This marriage, however, lasted for only about a year.

More about Tullia

Cicero's daughter Tullia was originally married to Piso (#2) (see below), but he died five years later, and she married a man named Furius Crassipes. For unknown reasons, that marriage ended, and when she wanted to marry a third time, she (and her mother) chose **Publius Cornelius Dolabella**, against her father's wishes. The marriage, apparently, was indeed unhappy, and their first child died in infancy. Tullia herself died while giving birth to a second child.

The World of Cicero

The first century B.C. was a period of huge growth for Rome, but also one of economic and military upheaval. Overseas conquests meant a great number of foreign captives; so small, family-run farms competed (often unsuccessfully) with larger operations based on slave labour. Small landowners had traditionally made up much of the Roman army, because they could provide their own weapons and sometimes horses; but with fewer of those landowners around, the militia now had to accept soldiers from the poorer classes, who had to be paid more so that they could afford weapons.

Rome, in Cicero's young years, also became a dangerous place, as power shifted back and forth between Gaius Marius and his former lieutenant Lucius Cornelius Sulla, and as political enemies were often punished by **proscription** (see **Top Vocabulary Terms**, below).

The Government of the Roman Republic

The Roman Empire did not formally exist until Octavius Caesar (later Caesar Augustus) became Emperor in 27 B.C. However, though it was still the era of the Roman Republic, Rome did have an empire because of the large amount of foreign territory it had acquired. For clarity, we will call it the small-e empire.

Social Classes

One class division was **family-based**, between the **patricians** (the nobility) and the **plebeians** (common people). There were also **property- or wealth-based classes** such as the *senatores*, who owned large amounts of land. The next level down, the **equestrian** class (in North's translation, the "knights of Rome"), was made up of those who could afford horses and who therefore made up the cavalry in times of war; this is the class to which Cicero's family belonged. There were also lower classes of property owners; and then, lowest of all, the proletarii (the "common people"). (Slaves didn't count as a class.)

Were the *senatores* the same as the senators?

Often, but the two were not identical. Over the centuries, and even within the Republic era, both the size of the Senate and the requirements for membership (such as age and wealth) changed. Some plebeians became senators along with the patricians. Those elected to **magistracies** (see below) were also included in the Senate.

What was an aedile, a quaestor, a consul, a censor?

The elected positions, or **magistracies**, in Rome included, starting at the bottom, **quaestor, aedile, praetor,** and **consul.** There were various numbers of each of these: for example, two consuls were elected each year. Ex-consuls could become censors; and a consul could become dictator if the need (usually a great emergency) arose. A **quaestor** was a treasurer. An **aedile** was the Roman official who oversaw public works (like the construction of buildings), and who was also responsible for public festivals. A **praetor** acted as governor of a province and also as a judge.

Censors were technically ranked below consuls and praetors, but the office was considered sacred and carried more dignity than that of the other magistracies. Two censors were elected for a period of five years, and they had to be chosen at the same time; if one censor died, the other had to step down as well, and two others would be chosen. There were often periods of time when there were no censors at all.

Who were the tribunes?

The duty of a non-military tribune (tribune of the plebeians, or tribune of the people) was to protect the common people from any individual or group (such as the nobles) who might attempt to suppress their rights. This position was not part of the junior-senior ranking of magistrates such as quaestor and consul; it was an office voted on by the common people.

People That Cicero Knew

Who was Pompey?

Gnaeus Pompeius Magnus, or Pompey the Great, was a Roman statesman and general, and the main rival of Julius Caesar.

Who Was Gaius Julius Caesar?

Julius Caesar was a political leader and general during the last days of the Roman Republic. Over his long career, he held every possible high civic, military, and even religious position in Rome.

Who was Young Caesar?

Gaius Octavius, or Octavian, later called Caesar Augustus, became the first roman Emperor in 27 B.C. **Not on translations of his name:** North uses "Octavius Caesar"; Dryden refers to him as "Young Caesar," or, later, just "Caesar." Other books, such as Genevieve Foster's *Augustus Caesar's World*, say "Octavian." For consistency, I have used "Octavius."

The Plutarch Project

Who was Brutus?

Marcus Junius Brutus the Younger, usually called Brutus; known for his part in the assassination of Julius Caesar in 44 B.C.; the subject of Plutarch's *Life of Marcus Brutus*.

People Named Piso

Lucius Calpurnius Piso Caesoninus (Piso #1) was a Roman senator, and consul in the year 58 B.C. along with Aulus Gabinius.

Gaius Calpurnius Piso Frugi (Piso #2) was the first husband of Cicero's daughter Tullia.

People named Lentulus

Publius Cornelius Lentulus Sura (Lentulus #1): a political agitator, executed for his role the Catiline conspiracy

Publius Cornelius Lentulus Spinther (Lentulus #2): consul 57 B.C.

Publius Cornelius Dolabella (the third husband of Tullia) was also known by his adoptive name **Lentulus (#3)**.

Other People whose names started with "C"

Cato: Marcus Porcius Cato Uticensis, or Cato the Younger, was a Roman statesman and the subject of one of Plutarch's *Lives*.

Catulus: Quintus Lutatius Catulus, censor along with Crassus in 65 B.C.

(Marcus Licinius) Crassus: a Roman general and politician (115 B.C.- 53 B.C.), one of the First Triumvirate with Caesar and Pompey; he was also known for his wealth.

Old School Friends

Cicero is known to have had at least three schoolmates who continued their friendship with him into adulthood. One of these early friends was **Gaius Marius Minor**, who was four years older than Cicero, and the son of a famous military commander—the **Marius** who was the chief rival to **Sulla**. ("Minor" is another way of saying "Junior" or "The Younger.") Marius Minor married the daughter of **Crassus**, and became a general himself. He was elected consul for 82 B.C., and fought against Sulla's forces, but was defeated, and committed suicide to avoid being captured by the enemy.

Another friend from school days was **Servius Sulpicius Rufus**, called Sulpicius, who was a year younger than Cicero. He became an expert in legal matters and was elected consul for 51 B.C. Sulpicius died while on a government mission in 43 B.C.

A third friend was **Titus Pomponius**, nicknamed "Atticus" (or "lover of Athens"), whose sister married Cicero's brother. Atticus was not a politician, but a businessman, first in Athens and, after 65 B.C., in Rome. He trained slaves to copy scrolls, and ran what we would call a publishing house (he published Cicero's books, among others). Atticus outlived the rest of the "gang," dying in 32 B.C.

Please note that, while all three were friends of Cicero, there is no actual evidence to suggest that they formed a close group together, during their school years or later on. But, if you can imagine that they did spend time together in their early years, this friendship is something that might have been carried on into their adult lives, and that idea is used for some of the **Creative Narrations**. (We might also add Cicero's younger brother, **Titus Quintus Cicero**, to the group.)

On the Map

Place names are listed under this heading. For consistency, I have used Dryden's spelling for places instead of North's. Charlotte Mason suggested using resources such as Dent's *Atlas of Ancient & Classical Geography*, which can be found online. A newer resource I have used myself is the *Historical Atlas of Ancient Rome* by Nick Constable (Checkmark Books/Thalamus Publishing, 2003).

Top Vocabulary Terms in the *Life of Cicero*

If you recognize these words, you are well on your way to mastering the vocabulary for this *Life*. They will not be repeated in the lessons.

1. **design:** plot, scheme (can be a noun or a verb)

2. **divers**: various, several

3. **drachmas, talents, myriads:** units of money, sometimes measured in weight rather than by specific coins.

4. **levy:** This usually means to gather up or enlist people (especially for military service). A second meaning of **levy** is to impose something on people, such as a tax. The word can be confused with **levee**, which refers to something rising (either an embankment that contains a river's rising, or an early-morning gathering).

5. **marketplace:** The open-air site called the **Forum** was the center of Roman business, political, and social life.

6. **meet:** When used as an adjective, it means proper, suitable. Other times it is used in its more common verb form: to meet someone.

7. **orator:** a professional public speaker. Orators used their skills to make political speeches (**orations**), or to defend or accuse someone in court (see **pleader**).

8. **pleaders, pleading, to plead:** All these refer to the practice of law, and students will recognize them in terms we still use: "Plead your case." "How do you plead?" Those doing the **pleading** at this time were generally the lawyers and orators, like Cicero.

9. **practise:** This can have two meanings: to practise something professionally (in Cicero's case, to participate in public life, **plead** cases, and make speeches); or to scheme and plot (in the same sense as **design**). Both meanings are used in this story. (A further note about the spelling of **practise**: in British/Canadian spelling, the verb is spelled with an s, *practise*, and the noun with a c, *practice*. In the U.S., both forms are spelled with a c.

10. **proscription:** an official condemnation, often of a group of people who were declared to be enemies of the state. Proscription could mean a death sentence, banishment and/or seizing of property.

11. **stay:** stop or delay. It can also be used in its more usual sense: "He went to stay in the country."

Lesson One

Introduction

In this lesson we are introduced to Cicero, who hoped "to make the name of the Ciceros noble and famous," and who signed his name with the symbol of a chickpea.

Vocabulary

fuller's shop: fulling is part of the processing of cloth

surname: a *cognomen*, or personal nickname; though in some cases (as with Cicero) it might be passed on through the family. Cicero's friend Titus Pomponius Atticus apparently chose his own surname.

rich pease: A *cicer* is a chickpea, a garbanzo bean. According to Plutarch, an ancestor of Cicero had a chickpea-shaped wart on his nose. Another theory is that he might have grown chickpeas. It was common for the Romans to have names that were, literally, "down to earth." In this story we hear of Piso (pea), and Lentulus (lentil); and there was also Fabius (bean). Cicero mentions the **Scauri** and **Catuli** families, but those names mean "swollen ankles" and "puppy," so perhaps they were not much more elevated than the "chickpeas."

made suit for office: ran for election

quaestor: the office of treasurer (see introductory notes)

pleasantly: jokingly

renowned: famous, respected

liberal sciences: or "liberal arts"; the scholarly subjects of the time, particularly arithmetic, astronomy, geometry, and music. As a side note, Cicero himself is the first writer known to have used the term "liberal arts," in a handbook he wrote for orators.

apter: more inclined, better at

extant at this day: still existing in Plutarch's time

commendation: praise

hath lost the name and estimation of it: is no longer so admired

Marsic War: also called the Social War; an uprising by former tribes of Italy who were demanding full Roman citizenship and rights

to a monarchy: Cicero saw that things were tending in that direction

sold by the crier: auctioned off

procured: got hold of, persuaded

in vehemence and heat of speaking: when he got excited

New Academy: a school of philosophy in Athens, founded by the successors of Plato

Stoics: those following a school of philosophy that taught, particularly, that one should endure pain and hardship without complaint

rhetoric: the art of effective and persuasive speech and writing

frame himself to be eloquent: prepare himself to be a good speaker

declaim: to make a speech

contended: competed

commiseration: sympathy, sorrow

People

Volscians: an ancient tribe of Italy whose people were eventually absorbed into Rome

Philo: Philo of Larissa, head of the Academy in Athens. He came to Rome in 87 B.C., and Cicero was one of those who eagerly attended his lectures.

Mucii: A prominent family of statesmen in Rome. **Quintus Mucius Scaevola Pontifex** wrote an eighteen-volume work on civil law. He was murdered during the struggle between **Sulla** and his rival **Gaius Marius** (the father of Cicero's friend Gaius Marius Minor—see note

72

in **Creative Narrations**).

Sulla: Lucius Cornelius Sulla Felix (c. 138 B.C.-78 B.C.) was a powerful Roman general and politician.

Antiochus of Ascalon: a philosopher who tried to reconcile the beliefs of the Skeptics and the Stoics.

Apollonius Molon: or Molo of Rhodes; a rhetorician

Posidonius: a Stoic philosopher

Historic Occasions

91-87 B.C.: Marsic or Social War (Cicero's early army experiences)

86 B.C.: Death of Gaius Marius (Senior), the main rival of Sulla

83-81 B.C.: Cicero began to practice as a lawyer

82 B.C.: Sulla ordered **proscriptions** against his enemies (see introductory notes).

82 B.C.: Death of Gaius Marius Minor (Junior)

80 B.C.: Cicero accused Chrysogonus of corruption (risking his safety under Sulla's rule)

79 B.C.: Cicero married Terentia (apparently before leaving for Greece)

79-77 B.C.: Cicero went to Greece and studied philosophy

78 B.C.: Death of Sulla, allowing Cicero to return safely to Rome

75 B.C.: Cicero was **quaestor** in Sicily (Plutarch is looking ahead here, as this story belongs to **Lesson Two**)

On the Map

Since this is an introductory lesson, it is important that students know something of Rome and its surroundings, as it was in the last years of the Republic, e.g. places such as Rome, Athens, Sicily, and Rhodes. Historical maps will show many of the (rapidly increasing) number of

Roman provinces: **Gaul**, **Syria**, **Asia**, etc. Many of the countries as we know them did not exist, or were made up of separate kingdoms or city-states. For example, Plutarch refers to **Italy**, but he means the mainland area that was not considered part of **Rome**. Similarly, he mentions that Cicero went to **Greece**, and the general meaning is the same, but much of Greece, at this time, belonged to the Roman province called **Achaia**. Achaia was considered a rather special province: it was not only a peaceful province (and therefore a choice assignment for Roman governors), but it was also considered a seat of education. In **Lesson One**, we read of Cicero studying in the city of **Athens**; and his son was later sent there for the same reason.

Reading

Part One

As touching Cicero's mother, whose name was Helvia, it is reported she was a gentlewoman born, and lived always very honestly: but for his father, the reports of him are diverse and infinite. For some say that he was born and brought up in a **fuller's shop**: others report that he came of Tullius Actius [or Attius], an illustrious king of the **Volscians**, who waged war, not without honour, against the Romans. But surely it seems to me, that the first of that name called Cicero, was some famous man, and that for his sake his offspring continued still that **surname**, and were glad to keep it, though many men scorned it, because *Cicer* in English signifieth a **rich pease**. That Cicero had a thing upon the tip of his nose, as it had been a little wart, much like to a rich pease, whereupon they surnamed him Cicero. But this Cicero, whose life we write of now, nobly answered certain of his friends on a time giving him counsel to change his name, when he first **made suit for office**, and began to practise in matters of state: that he would endeavour himself to make the name of the Ciceros more noble and famous than the Scauri, or Catuli. And when he was **quaestor** in Sicily, he gave an offering of certain silver plate unto the gods, and at large engraved on it his two first names, Marcus Tullius: and in place of his third name, he **pleasantly** commanded the workman to cut out the form and fashion of a rich pease. Thus much they write of his name.

Now for his birth, it was said that his mother was brought abed of him without any pain, the third day of January, the same day on which now the magistrates of Rome pray and sacrifice for the emperor. It is said, also, that a vision appeared to his nurse, which foretold that he should afterwards do great good unto all the Romans. Now though such things may seem but dreams and fables unto many, yet Cicero himself shortly after proved this prophecy true. For as soon as he was of an age to begin to have lessons, he became so distinguished for his talent, and got such a name and reputation amongst the boys, that their fathers would often visit the school that they might see young Cicero, and might be able to say that they themselves had witnessed the quickness and readiness in learning for which he was **renowned**. But others of the rude and baser sort of men were offended with their sons, because to honour Cicero, they did always put him in the midst between them, as they went in the streets.

Cicero indeed had such a natural wit and understanding, as Plato thought meet for learning, and apt for the study of philosophy. For he gave himself to all kinds of knowledge, and there was no art, nor any of the **liberal sciences**, that he disdained: notwithstanding in his first young years he was **apter**, and better disposed to the study of poetry, than any other. There is a pretty poem of his in verses of eight staves, called "Pontius Glaucus," **extant at this day**, which he made when he was but a boy. After that, being given more earnestly unto this study, he was not only thought the best orator, but the best poet also of all the Romans in his time: and yet doth the excellency of his eloquence, and **commendation** of his tongue continue, even to this day, notwithstanding the great alteration and change of the Latin tongue. But his poetry **hath lost the name and estimation of it**, because there were many after him that became far more excellent therein than he.

Part Two

After he had left his childish studies, he became then a scholar of **Philo**, the Academic philosopher *[omission]*. He gave himself also to be a follower of the **Mucii**, who were eminent statesmen and leaders in the Senate, and acquired from them a knowledge of the laws.. He did also follow **Sulla** for a time, in the **Marsic war**. But when he saw that the commonwealth of Rome fell to civil wars, and from civil wars **to a monarchy**: then he returned again to his book and contemplative life, and studied with the learned men of Greece *[omission]*.

About that time, **Sulla** causing the goods of one that was said to be have been put to death by proscription, to be **sold by the crier**: Chrysogonus, one of Sulla's freed slaves, and in great favour with his master, bought them for the sum of two thousand drachmas. And when Roscius, the son and heir of the dead, complained, and demonstrated the estate to be worth two hundred and fifty talents, Sulla took it angrily to have his actions questioned, and **procured** Chrysogonus to accuse him (Roscius), that he had killed his own father. Never an orator dared speak in Roscius' behalf to defend his cause, but shrunk in fear, fearing Sulla's cruelty and severity.

The young man, being thus deserted, came for refuge to Cicero. Cicero's friends encouraged him, saying he was not likely ever to have a fairer and more honourable introduction to public life. Thereupon Cicero determined to take his cause in hand, and did handle it so well, that he obtained the thing he sued for: whereby he won him great fame and credit. But fearing Sulla, he travelled into Greece, and gave it out that he did so for the benefit of his health. Indeed Cicero was dog-lean, a little eater, and would also eat late, because of the great weakness of his stomach. His voice was loud and good, but so harsh and unmanaged that **in vehemence and heat of speaking** he always raised it to so high a tone that there seemed to be reason to fear about his health.

When he came to Athens, he went to hear **Antiochus of Ascalon**, and fell in great liking with his sweet tongue, and excellent grace, though otherwise he misliked his new opinions in philosophy. For Antiochus had now fallen off from the **New Academy**, as they call it [omission], and in most things had embraced the doctrine of the **Stoics**. But Cicero rather affected and adhered to the doctrines of the New Academy; and did study that sect more than all the rest, of purpose: so that if he were forbidden to practise in the commonwealth at Rome, he would then go to Athens (leaving all pleas and orators in the commonwealth) to bestow the rest of his time quietly in the study of philosophy.

Part Three

At length, when he heard news of Sulla's death, and saw that his body was grown to good state and health by exercise, and that his voice became daily more and more to fill men's ears with a sweet and pleasant sound, and yet was loud enough for the constitution of his body; receiving letters daily from his friends at Rome, that prayed him to return home, and moreover, Antiochus himself also earnestly persuading him to practise in the commonwealth: he began again to fall to the study of **rhetoric**, and to **frame himself to be eloquent**, being a necessary thing for an orator, and did continually exercise himself in making orations upon any speech or proposition, and so frequented the chief orators and masters of eloquence that were at that time. He sailed from Athens for **Asia** and **Rhodes** *[omission];* at Rhodes, he studied oratory with **Apollonius Molon**, and philosophy with **Posidonius**.

Apollonius, we are told, not understanding Latin, requested Cicero to **declaim** in Greek. He complied willingly, thinking that his faults would thus be better pointed out to him. And after he finished, all his other hearers were astonished, and **contended** who should praise him most, but Apollonius, who had shown no signs of excitement whilst he was hearing him, so also now, when it was over, sat musing for some considerable time, without any remark. And when Cicero was discomposed at this, he said, "You have my praise and admiration, Cicero, and Greece my pity and **commiseration**, since those arts and that eloquence which are the only glories that remain to her, will now be transferred by you to Rome."

Narration and Discussion

Describe the early life of Cicero. What were the biggest influences on his character?

What was Cicero's particular reason for studying Greek philosophy?

Creative narration #1: Have you ever made a timeline of your own life story so far? "I started school," "We moved," "I won a music prize" are things students typically include. Create a timeline of Cicero's life from birth to age 30, illustrating it as you like. (You may have to guess at some of the years.)

Creative narration #2, for older students: In the introductory notes for the study, please read the section **Old School Friends**, which describes three of Cicero's schoolmates and their later lives. One of them, Gaius Marius Minor, died during the period covered by this lesson. Write a letter from one of the three remaining friends to another, mentioning recent events. (**Note:** This, and other **Old School Friends** activities, are suggested for older students, not because the activities themselves are difficult, but because students wanting to find out more about people or events may land on inappropriate websites.)

For older students and further thought: Philo was an **Academic Skeptic**, and taught that, although truth existed, humans were not capable of fully comprehending or distinguishing it; the best one could do was form a sort of doubtful belief and act on that. **Stoic** philosophers, on the other hand, believed that, while not everything was true, there were nevertheless some truths which could be well grasped, often through one's senses. What do the Christian scriptures teach about our ability to discern truth? Can what we experience (see, hear, touch) in the physical world indeed help us to understand more abstract ideas? (Consider Psalm 8.)

Lesson Two

Introduction

When Cicero returned to Rome, he quickly became someone to watch, as he began to move up the government ranks. He was elected to the office of quaestor, then aedile; and he had "many men daily at his gate every morning." Even Pompey the Great came to ask his advice.

Vocabulary

full of expectations: confident; expecting to be successful

oracle: a Greek prophecy (when Cicero had not yet returned to Rome). Plutarch refers to the **god of Delphi** or Apollo, who was believed to be responsible for these **oracles**, and the **Pythia** or **Pythoness**, who was the priestess at **Delphi** responsible for delivering the messages.

blunted the edge of his inclination: discouraged him a bit

his own genius: This does not refer to intellectual ability, but to one's inner guide or spirit; we might say "his own calling."

backward in pretending to public offices: he held back from trying to be elected for anything; we might say he was flying under the radar

Atreus deliberating the revenge of his brother Thyestes: a story from Greek mythology

scepter: an ornamented staff, the symbol of a king (i.e. **Atreus**)

it did not a little contribute to render his eloquence persuasive: it actually helped his rhetorical skills quite a bit

corn: grain such as wheat or barley

fell to his lot: as quaestor, he was also expected to assist the governor of a province outside of Rome, in this case Sicily

lenity: gentleness, mercy

praetor: an official who acted as governor of a province and as a judge.

acquitted: found not guilty

ludicrous: This usually means "ridiculous," but a better word here might be simply "amusing."

artificers and craftsmen: artisans, tradespeople

negligent: neglectful

eminent: prominent, highly respected

he should not have daylight: he would not have time before the court closed (and it was the last possible day)

jointure: dowry (money given on marriage by the bride's family)

myriads of denarii: another money term (that apparently came into use due to rising inflation!)

nice and delicate: extremely careful, picky

pay court to: pay special attention to

People

Roscius the comedian: an actor of comic plays

Aesop the tragedian: Clodius Aesopus, an actor of tragedies

Terentia: Cicero's wife; see introductory notes

Marcus Licinius Crassus, called Crassus: see introductory notes

Gnaeus Pompeius Magnus, called Pompey: see introductory notes

Historic Occasions

75 B.C.: Cicero was **quaestor** in Sicily (An interesting point: Cicero attained each of his positions at or near the youngest allowable age; for example, the minimum age for a quaestor was 30.)

69 B.C.: Cicero became **aedile**

On the Map

Sicily: the large island at the toe of Italy's "boot," which was now the Roman province of **Sicilia**

Campania: a region of southwestern Italy; its capital city is **Naples**

Arpi: a city in **Apulia**

Pompeii: a city located near **Naples** (until in 79 A.D.)

near the Palatine Hill: The Palatine Hill was centermost of the Seven Hills of Rome, and one of the oldest and wealthiest parts of the city.

Reading

Part One

And now when Cicero, **full of expectations**, was again bent upon

80

political affairs, a certain **oracle blunted the edge of his inclination**; for consulting the **god of Delphi** how he should attain most glory, the **Pythoness** answered "by making **his own genius** and not the opinion of the people the guide of his life"; and therefore at first he passed his time in Rome cautiously, and was very **backward in pretending to public offices**, so that he was at that time in little esteem, and had got the nicknames, so readily given by low and ignorant people in Rome, of "Greek" and "Scholar." But when his own desire of fame and the eagerness of his father and relations had made him take in earnest to pleading, he made no slow or gentle advance to the first place, but so soon as he fell to practise, he was immediately esteemed above all the other orators and pleaders in his time, and did excel them all.

At first, it is said, he (like Demosthenes) was defective in his delivery, and on that account he paid much attention to the instructions, sometimes of **Roscius the comedian**, and sometimes of **Aesop the tragedian**. They tell of this Aesop, that whilst he was playing **Atreus deliberating the revenge of his brother Thyestes**, he was so transported beyond himself in the heat of action, that he struck with his **scepter** one of the servants, who was running across the stage, so violently that he laid him dead upon the place. And such afterwards was Cicero's delivery that **it did not a little contribute to render his eloquence persuasive**. He used to ridicule loud speakers, saying that they shouted because they could not speak *[omission]*. Truly pleasant taunts do grace an orator, and show a fine wit: but yet Cicero used them so commonly, that they were offensive unto many, and brought him to be counted a malicious scoffer and spiteful man.

Part Two

He was appointed quaestor when there was great scarcity of **corn** at Rome, and the province of **Sicily fell to his lot**. At his first coming thither, the Sicilians misliked him very much, because he compelled them to send corn unto Rome: but after they had found his diligence, justice, and **lenity**, they honoured him above any governor that ever was sent from Rome. It happened, also, that some young Romans of good and noble families, charged with neglect of discipline and misconduct in military service, were brought before the **praetor** in Sicily. Cicero undertook their defense, which he conducted admirably, and got them **acquitted**.

So returning to Rome with a great opinion of himself for these things, a **ludicrous** incident befell him, as he tells us himself. Meeting an eminent citizen in **Campania**, whom he accounted his friend, he asked him what the Romans said and thought of his actions, as if the whole city had been filled with the glory of what he had done. His friend asked him again: "And where hast thou been, Cicero, all this while, that we have not seen thee at Rome?" This killed his heart straight, when he saw that the report of his name and doings, entering into the city of Rome as into an infinite sea, was so suddenly vanquished away again, without any other fame or speech. But after that, when he looked into himself, and saw that in reason he took an infinite labour in hand to attain to glory, wherein he saw no certain end whereby to attain unto it: it cut off a great part of the ambition he had in his head. And yet the great pleasure he took to hear his own praise, and continued to the very last to be passionately fond of glory: those two things continued with him even to his dying day, and did later make him swerve from justice.

Part Three

On beginning to apply himself more resolutely to public business, he thought it an ill thing that **artificers and craftsmen** should have many sorts of instruments and tools without life, to know the names of every one of them, the places where they should take them, and the use whereto they should employ them: and yet that a man of knowledge and quality (who doth all things with the help and service of men) should be **negligent** and careless in the knowledge of persons. And so he not only acquainted himself with the names, but also knew the particular places where every one of the more **eminent** citizens dwelt, what lands he possessed, the friends he made use of, and those that were of his neighbourhood, and when he travelled on any road in Italy, he could readily name and show the estates and seats of his friends and acquaintance.

He was not very rich, and yet he had enough to serve his turn: the which made men muse the more at him, and they loved him the better, because he took no fee nor gift for his pleading, what cause soever he had in hand, and more especially that he did not do so when he undertook the prosecution of Verres. This Verres had been praetor of Sicily, and had committed many evil practices there, for the which the Sicilians did accuse him. Cicero, taking upon him to defend their cause, made Verres to be condemned, not by speaking, but in a manner by holding his tongue. The praetors being his judges, and favouring Verres, had made so many adjournments and delays, that they had driven it off to the last day of hearing. Cicero perceiving then **he should not have daylight** to speak all that he had to say against him, and that thereby nothing should be done and judged: he rose up, and said there was no need of speeches; and after producing and examining witnesses, he required the judges to proceed to sentence.

[omission of certain "witty sayings" made during the trial]

In the end, Verres was convicted; though Cicero, who set the fine at seventy-five myriads, lay under the suspicion of being corrupted by bribery to lessen the sum. But the Sicilians, in testimony of their gratitude, came and brought him all sorts of presents from the island, when he was aedile; of which he made no private profit himself, but used their generosity only to reduce the public price of provisions.

Part Four

Cicero had a very pleasant seat at **Arpi**; he had also a farm near **Naples**, and another about **Pompeii**; but neither of any great value. Afterwards also he had the **jointure** of his wife **Terentia**, which amounted to the sum of twelve myriads (*Dryden says ten*), and besides all this, he had a bequest valued at nine **myriads of denarii**; upon those he lived in a liberal but temperate style with the learned Greeks and Romans that were his familiars He rarely, if at any time, sat down to meat till sunset, and that not so much on account of business, as for his health and the weakness of his stomach. He was otherwise in the care of his body **nice and delicate**, appointing himself, for example, a set number of walks and rubbings. And after this manner managing the habit of his body, he brought it in time to be healthful, and capable of supporting many great fatigues and trials.

His father's house he made over to his brother, living himself **near the Palatine Hill**, because such as came to wait upon him to do him honour, should not take the pains to go so far to see him. For he had as many men daily at his gate every morning, as either **Crassus** had for his wealth, or **Pompey** for his estimation among the soldiers, both of them being at that time the chiefest men of Rome. Nay, even Pompey himself used to **pay court to** Cicero, and Cicero's public actions did much to establish Pompey's authority and reputation in the state.

Narration and Discussion

How did Cicero work to improve his speaking ability? How did he take things a bit too far?

Discuss this sentence: "And yet the great pleasure he took to hear his own praise, and continued to the very last to be passionately fond of glory: those two things continued with him even to his dying day, and did eftsoons make him swerve from justice."

For older students or those wishing to go deeper: "He used to ridicule loud speakers, saying that they shouted because they could not speak…" What did Cicero mean? Why is it sometimes more difficult to speak quietly, or write simply?

Creative narration: Choose a scene from this reading to act out (but not Aesop's portrayal of Atreus).

Lesson Three

Introduction

"At that time many men practised to subvert the government, not for the benefit of the commonwealth, but to serve their own covetous minds."

The next four lessons deal with the **Second Catiline (or Catilinarian) Conspiracy**, an uprising that took place in 63 B.C. This was a time of economic hardship for both city dwellers and rural people. One of the problems was that public land that could have been used for family farms was being bought up by commercial growers. Many formerly rich people were in debt because of lavish personal spending and gambling. Also on the list of unhappy Romans were veteran soldiers who had fought under Sulla. But in this lesson, we hear only rumblings of trouble.

Vocabulary

extortion: taking something, especially money, by force

quit of his accusation: found not guilty

and never rose after: it is implied that he committed suicide

peculation: stealing money

put in suit: brought to court

to despite Pompey with: to annoy or get back at Pompey

with equity and humanity: respectfully and fairly

studiously appointed: carefully chosen

he made a notable oration: This was a tricky situation, because Cicero was trying to please several different groups of people at once; but he did defend Manilius, and kept his favour with the Roman people.

preferred to: chosen for

consul: see introductory notes

subvert the government: overthrow the government

covetous: selfish, greedy

seditious: rebellious

impetus: force that sets something in motion

contention: disagreement, quarreling

a commission of ten persons, the Decemviri: a group of ten rulers

like a hired player: like an actor on the stage

People

Licinius Macer: a former tribune and praetor

Manilius [sometimes spelled Manlius]: Gaius Manilius, a tribune.

Lucius Sergius Catilina: also called **Catiline** in English; a politician of the patrician (upper) class, best known for the **Catilinarian** or **Catiline Conspiracy**, a series of attempts to overthrow the government of Rome

Gaius Antonius, called **Antonius:** Gaius Antonius Hybrida, co-consul with Cicero in 63 B.C.; uncle of the famous **Mark Antony**.

Historic Occasions

66 B.C.: Cicero became praetor; the events with Licinius Macer

65 B.C.: Cicero's friend Atticus returned to Rome from Athens

64 B.C.: Catiline ran for the office of consul (for 63 B.C.), but Cicero was elected instead

On the Map

Pontus: a region on the southern coast of the **Black Sea**, part of present-day Turkey. It was annexed to the Roman empire in 64 B.C.

Armenia: an ancient kingdom which came under Roman rule in 66 B.C.

Tuscany: a region of central Italy

Gaul: The term "Gaul" covers, literally, a great deal of ground north of Italy, including regions on each side of the **Alps**.

Reading

Part One

Numerous distinguished competitors stood with him for the praetor's office, yet was he first chosen before them all; and he did so honestly behave himself in that office, that they did not so much as once suspect him of bribery or **extortion**. And for proof hereof, it is reported, that **Licinius Macer** (a man that of himself was of great power, and yet favoured and supported besides by Crassus) was accused before Cicero of theft and extortion in his office; but he, trusting much to his supposed credit, and to the great suit and labour his friends made for him, Licinius went home to his house before sentence proceeded against him (the judges being yet to give their opinions), and there speedily trimmed his beard, and put a new gown upon his back, as though he had been sure to have been **quit of his accusation**, and then returned again into the marketplace. But Crassus went to meet him, and told him all the judges had condemned him. Licinius Macer took such a grief and conceit upon it, that he went home to his house again, laid him down on his bed, **and never rose after**. This judgement won Cicero great fame, for they praised him exceedingly for the great pains he took to see justice duly executed.

[omission of another case]

Towards the end of his office, two or three days before his time expired, **Manilius** was brought before him, and charged with **peculation**. This Manilius was very well beloved of the common people, who were persuaded that he was **put in suit** not for any fault he had committed, but only **to despite Pompey with**, whose familiar friend he was. So he required certain days to answer the matter he was accused of; but Cicero would give him no further respite, but [required him] to answer it the next day. The people therewith were marvellously offended, because the other praetors in such cases were accustomed to give ten days' respite to others.

The next morning when the tribunes had brought him before the judges, and also accused him unto them: he besought Cicero to hear him patiently. Cicero said that as he had always treated the accused **with equity and humanity**, as far as the law allowed, so he thought it hard to deny the same to Manilius, and that he had **studiously appointed** that day of which alone, as praetor, he was master; and that it was not the part of those that were desirous to help him to cast the judgment of his cause upon another praetor. These words did marvellously change the peoples' opinion and affection towards him, and every man speaking well of him, they prayed him to defend Manilius' cause. He willingly granted it to them: and coming from the bench, standing at the bar like an orator to plead for him, **he made a notable oration**, and spoke both boldly and sharply against the chief men of the city and on those who were jealous of Pompey.

Part Two

Yet he was **preferred to** the **consulship** no less by the nobles than the common people, for the good of the city; and both parties jointly assisted his promotion upon the following reasons. The change and alteration of government, which Sulla brought in, was thought strange at the first among the people: but now men by process of time being used to it, it was thoroughly established, and no man misliked it. At that time many men practised to **subvert the government**, not for the benefit of the commonwealth, but to serve their own **covetous** minds. For Pompey being then in the east parts, made wars with the kings of **Pontus** and **Armenia**, and had not left sufficient force at Rome to oppress these **seditious** persons that sought nothing but rebellion. These men had made **Lucius Catiline** their captain: a desperate man who would attempt any great enterprise, subtle, and malicious of nature.

[a "wise and necessary omission" about the nasty vices of Catiline]

Furthermore all **Tuscany** began to revolt, and the most part of **Gaul** also, lying **between the Alps and Italy**. The city of Rome itself was also in great danger of an uprising, on account of the unequal distribution of wealth and property, those of highest rank and greatest spirit having impoverished themselves by shows, entertainments, ambition of offices, and sumptuous buildings, and the riches of the city having thus fallen into the hands of mean men and low-born persons. So that there wanted but a slight **impetus** to set all in motion, it being in the power of every daring man to overturn a sickly commonwealth.

Catiline, however, being desirous of procuring a strong position to carry out his designs, stood for the consulship, and had great hopes of success, thinking he should be appointed, with Gaius Antonius as his colleague, who was a man fit to lead neither in a good cause nor in a bad one, but might be a valuable accession to another's power. Divers noble and wise men foreseeing that, did procure Cicero to sue for the consulship. The people accepted him, and rejected Catiline. Antonius and Cicero thereupon were created consuls, although Cicero, of all the suitors for the consulship, was but only of the equestrian class and not of the *senatores*.

Part Three

Though the designs of Catiline were not yet publicly known, even at the beginning of Cicero's consulship there fell out great trouble and **contention** in the commonwealth. For, one the one side, those who were disqualified by the laws of Sulla from holding any public offices (who were no small men, neither few in number) began to creep into the people's goodwill, speaking many things truly and justly against the tyranny of Sulla, only that they disturbed the government at an improper and unseasonable time. On the other hand, the tribunes of the people proposed laws to the same purpose, constituting **a commission of ten persons**, with unlimited powers, in whom as supreme governors should be vested the right of selling the public lands of all Italy and Syria, and also through all the countries and provinces which Pompey had newly conquered to the empire of Rome: to sell, and release all the lands belonging to the state of Rome, to accuse any man whom they thought good, to banish any man, to restore the colonies with people, to take what money they would out of the treasury, to levy men of war, and to keep them in pay as long as they thought good.

For this great and absolute power of **the Decemviri**, there were many men of great account that favoured this law, but chiefly Antonius, being colleague and fellow consul with Cicero, for he had good hope to be chosen one of these ten commissioners; and furthermore, it was thought that he was privy unto Catiline's conspiracy, and that he misliked it not, because he was so much in debt. And this [his being chosen as one of the ten] was the thing that the noblemen most feared. Thereupon Cicero, [in an attempt] to prevent this danger, granted Antonius [the governorship of] Macedonia; and the province of Gaul being offered unto himself, he refused it. And this piece of favour so completely won over Antonius, that he was ready to second and respond to, **like a hired player**, whatever Cicero said for the good of the country. And now, having made his colleague thus tame and tractable, he could with greater courage attack the conspirators.

And therefore, in the Senate, making an oration against the law of the ten commissioners, he so confounded those who proposed it, that they had nothing to reply. And when they again endeavoured, and, having prepared things beforehand, had called the consuls before the assembly of the people, Cicero, fearing nothing, went first out, and commanded the Senate to follow him, and not only succeeded in throwing out the law, but so entirely overpowered the tribunes by his oratory [North: he struck them so dead with his eloquence] that they abandoned all thought of their other projects.

For Cicero only, of all men in Rome, made the Romans know how much eloquence doth grace and beautify that which is honest, and how invincible right and justice are, being eloquently set forth; and also how that a man that will be counted a wise governor of a commonwealth, should always in his doings rather prefer profit, than to seek to curry favour with the common people: yet so to use his words, that the thing which is profitable may not be also unpleasant.

[omission for length]

Narration and Discussion

Describe the growing threat of rebellion that began to be felt in Rome. What were some of the problems?

Why did Cicero refuse the governorship of Gaul? Wouldn't he have been pleased to be given such an honour?

Creative narration #1: Cicero wanted "to use his words, that the thing which is profitable may not be also unpleasant." Find a way in which you can do that today.

Creative narration #2: Continue the **Old School Friends** narration activity suggested in **Lesson One**. As **Atticus** would have recently returned to Rome, perhaps the group could have a reunion (and discuss current events). This could be a written or dramatic activity.

For further thought (for older students): Discuss this sentence: "For Cicero only of all men in Rome made the Romans know, how much eloquence doth grace and beautify that which is honest, and how invincible right and justice are, being eloquently set forth..."

Lesson Four

Introduction

After an early, failed attempt at rebellion (the First Catiline Conspiracy, not described here by Plutarch), the supporters of Catiline began to rise again, with a plan that included "an unfortunate but fatal accident to Cicero." But Catiline's hope of election as consul was ended when two others were chosen. The Second Conspiracy came to a head when incriminating documents were mysteriously brought to Cicero's door, and Catiline was ejected from Rome (but not beaten yet).

Vocabulary

cowed and disheartened : frightened and discouraged

spoil and ransack: loot, take what they pleased

the tumult and hurly burly: the chaos of the elections

manifest conjectures and proofs: many opinions and suppositions

deferring: postponing

audacious: bold. North translates it as "gentle," but that seems to be incorrect.

Field of Mars: the *Campus Martius*, a large open area used as a parade ground or for other public events

discovered: revealed

91

subscribed: signed

according to their direction: to those who were to receive the letters

bewray: divulge, betray

gaping: waiting with bated breath

refer the care of the commonwealth unto the consuls; absolute authority: giving the consuls power to do whatever they believed was necessary in this emergency situation

a time of present fear and danger: There is an interesting similarity here to the U.S. Supreme Court phrase "clear and present danger."

betimes: early

chafe and rail: make a fuss

temple of Jupiter Stator: a temple in the *Campus Martius*

axes and bundles of rods: the *fasces*, carried by Roman guards (*lictors*) mainly to symbolize the power of a magistrate, but occasionally for practical purposes as well.

People

Silanus: Decimus Junius Silanus, one of the consuls elected for 62 B.C.

Murena: Lucius Licinius Murena, the other consul

Quintus Metellus: Quintus Caecilius Metellus Celer, the brother-in-law of Pompey; he became consul in 60 B.C.

Historic Occasions

63 B.C.: Cicero's year as consul.

63 B.C.: The Second Catiline Conspiracy

63 B.C.: the birth of Octavius (Caesar Augustus), which Cicero later took as a good omen

On the Map

Etruria: a region of central Italy

Reading

Part One

The conspirators with Catiline, at first **cowed and disheartened**, began presently to take courage again. And assembling themselves together, they exhorted one another boldly to undertake the design before Pompey's return, who was said to be on the way towards Rome with his army.

But besides them, those soldiers that had served before in the wars under Sulla, being dispersed up and down Italy (but specially the best soldiers among them dwelling in the cities of **Etruria**) did stir up Catiline to hasten the enterprise, persuading themselves that they should once again have goods enough at hand to **spoil and ransack** at their pleasure. These soldiers having Manilius as their captain, that had borne office in the field under Sulla, conspired with Catiline, and came to Rome to assist him in his suit: who purposed once again to demand the consulship, being determined at the election to kill Cicero in **the tumult and hurly burly**. The gods also did plainly show by earthquakes, lightning and thunder, and by vision of spirits that did appear, the secret practise and conspiracy: besides also, there fell out **manifest conjectures and proofs** by men that came to reveal them, though not sufficient for the conviction of the noble and powerful Catiline.

Cicero therefore **deferring** the day of election, called Catiline into the Senate, and there did examine him of that which was reported of him. Catiline supposing there were many in the Senate that had goodwills to rebel, and also because he would show himself ready unto them that were of his conspiracy, returned an **audacious** answer. "What harm," said he, "when I see two bodies, the one lean and rotten with a head, the other great and strong without one, if I put a head to that body which wants one?" He meant, under this dark answer, to signify the people and the Senate.

This answer being made, Cicero was more afraid than before,

insomuch that he put on armour for the safety of his body, and was accompanied with the chiefest men of Rome, and a great number of young men besides, going with him from his house unto the **Field of Mars,** where the elections were made. Here, designedly letting his tunic slip partly off from his shoulders, he showed his armour underneath, and **discovered** his danger to the spectators. Every man misliked it when they saw it, and came about him to defend him, if any offered to assail him. But it so came to pass, that by voices of the people, Catiline was again rejected from the consulship, and **Silanus** and **Murena** were chosen consuls.

Part Two

Not long after this, Catiline's soldiers got together in a body in Etruria, and began to form themselves into companies, the day appointed for the design being near at hand. About midnight, there came three of the chiefest men of Rome to Cicero's house: Marcus Crassus, Marcus Marcellus, and Scipio Metellus). Knocking at his gate, they called his porter, and bade him wake his master presently, and tell him how they three were at the gate to speak with him, about a matter of importance. At night after supper, Crassus' porter had brought his master a packet of letters, delivered him by a stranger unknown, which were directed unto divers persons, among the which one of them had no name **subscribed**, but was only directed unto Crassus himself. The effect of his letter was, that there should be a great slaughter in Rome made by Catiline, and therefore he prayed him that he would depart out of Rome to save himself. Crassus having read his own letter, would not open the rest, but went forthwith unto Cicero, partly for fear of the danger, and partly also to clear himself of the suspicion they had of him for the friendship that was betwixt him and Catiline.

Cicero counselling with them what was to be done, the next morning assembled the Senate very early, and carrying the letters with him, he did deliver them **according to their direction**, and commanded they should read them out aloud. All these letters, and every one of them particularly, did **bewray** the conspiracy. Furthermore, Quintus Arrius, a man of authority, and that had been praetor, told openly about the soldiers and men of war collecting in companies in Etruria. And it was reported also, that Manilius was in the field with a great number of soldiers about the cities of Tuscany, **gaping** daily to hear news of some change at Rome. All these things being thoroughly considered, a decree passed by the Senate, that they should **refer the care of the commonwealth unto the consuls** [Cicero and Antonius], to the end that with **absolute authority** they might (as well as they could) provide for the safety and preservation thereof. Such manner of decree and authority, was not often seen concluded of in the Senate, but in **a time of present fear and danger**.

After Cicero had received this power, he committed all affairs outside to **Quintus Metellus**, but the management of the city he kept in his own hands. Such a numerous attendance guarded him every day when he went abroad, that the greatest part of the marketplace was filled with his train when he entered it.

Catiline, impatient of further delay, resolved himself to break forth and go to Manilius, where their army lay. But before he departed, he had drawn into his confederacy one Martius, and another called Cethegus, whom he commanded to go early in the morning to Cicero's house with short daggers to kill him, pretending to come to salute him, and to give him a good morrow. But there was a noblewoman of Rome, called Fulvia, who went overnight unto Cicero, and bade him beware of that Cethegus, who indeed came the next morning **betimes** unto him: but being denied to be let in, he began to **chafe and rail** before the gate. This made him the more to be suspected.

In the end Cicero coming out of his house, called the Senate to the **temple of Jupiter Stator**, which standeth at the upper end of the Sacred Street, going up to the Palatine. There was Catiline with others, as though he meant to clear himself of the suspicion that went of him: howbeit there was not a senator that would sit down by him, but they did all rise from the bench where Catiline had taken his place. And further, when he began to speak, he could have no audience for the great noise they made against him. So at length Cicero rose, and commanded him to leave the city: saying, that there must needs be a separation of walls between them two, considering that the one used but words, and the other force of arms. Catiline thereupon immediately departing the city with three hundred armed men, was no sooner out of the precinct of the walls, but he made his sergeants carry **axes and bundles of rods** before him, as if he had been a consul lawfully created, and did display his ensigns of war, and so went in this order to seek Manilius. And having got together a body of near twenty thousand men, with these he marched to the several cities, endeavouring to persuade or force them to revolt.

So it being now come to open war, Antonius (Cicero's colleague and fellow consul) was sent forth to fight him.

Narration and Discussion

If so many people suspected Catiline of conspiring to overthrow the government, why couldn't they just arrest him?

Why did the Romans "mislike" to see Cicero wearing armour under his outer clothing? Weren't they glad to see he was protected?

When the senators heard the proof of the conspiracy, how did they react?

Creative narration #1: Act as a newspaper or television reporter, and tell about what has been happening in Rome.

Creative narration #2 (for older students): Continue the **Old School Friends** activity suggested in **Lesson One**, writing a letter (or a series of letters) from one of the friends to another.

Lesson Five

Introduction

Pompey's army was on its way back to Rome, meaning that any attempt to take over the government had to be carried out immediately. Catiline had been banished from the city (and was building an army elsewhere), but his supporters came up with a desperate plan involving fire, murder, and kidnapping. The plot was uncovered and the conspirators were arrested. However, this meant that Cicero had to make an on-the-spot decision about their fate.

Vocabulary

debauchery: immorality

designed no mean or trivial matter: planned something really big

reserve for pledges: hold as hostages

Saturnalia: a Roman festival, held for several nights in December

flax and sulfur: materials for starting a fire, possibly to be used as incendiary arrows

Temple of Concord: a temple to the goddess Concordia, which was often used for Senate meetings

consorts: confederates; friends

the feast of the goddess whom the Romans call the Good: this is the same ceremony that Clodius later disrupted at Caesar's house (**Lesson Seven**)

their deserts: what they deserved

amend: mend their ways

timorous: fearful

dissemble: conceal the truth

People

Publius Cornelius Lentulus (#1), surnamed Sura: a conspirator with Catiline

Gaius Caesar: Gaius Julius Caesar

Cato: Cato the Younger, an influential statesman and orator of that time. He called Cicero "the father of his country."

Historic Occasions

75 B.C. Publius Cornelius Lentulus Sura was praetor (first time)

74 B.C.: Lentulus was governor of Sicily

71 B.C.: Lentulus was consul

70 B.C.: Lentulus was expelled from the Senate

63 B.C.: Lentulus was elected praetor (second time)

December 63 B.C.: Lentulus and other conspirators were arrested

On the Map

the **Allobroges:** one of the tribes of **Gaul** (to the north)

Reading

Part One

The remainder of those in the city whom he had corrupted, **Publius Cornelius Lentulus (#1)** kept together and encouraged. He had the surname **Sura**, and was of a noble family, but for his **debauchery** had been turned out of the Senate. He was now holding the office of praetor for the second time, as the custom is with those who desire to regain the dignity of senator.

[Omission for length: how Lentulus got his nickname "Sura."]

This man, such in his own nature, and now inflamed by Catiline, false prophets and fortune-tellers had also corrupted with vain hopes, quoting to him fictitious verses and oracles, and proving from the Sibylline prophecies that there were three of the name Cornelius designed by fate to be monarchs of Rome; two of whom, Cinna and Sulla, had already fulfilled the decree, and that divine fortune was now advancing with the gift of monarchy for the remaining third "Cornelius"; and that therefore he ought by all means to accept it, and not lose opportunity by delay, as Catiline had done. He therefore **designed no mean or trivial matter**, but intended to kill the whole Senate, and as many other citizens as they could murder, and to set fire to Rome, sparing none but Pompey's sons, whom they would **reserve**

for pledges, to make their peace afterwards with Pompey. (For the rumor was very great and certain also, that Pompey had returned from very great wars and conquests which he had made in the Eastern countries.)

The night appointed for the design was one of the **Saturnalia**. Swords, **flax, and sulfur** they carried and hid in the house of Cethegus; and providing one hundred men, and dividing the city into as many parts, they had allotted to every one singly his proper place, so that in a moment, many kindling the fire, the city might be in a flame all together. Other men also were appointed to stop the pipes and water conduits which brought water to Rome, and to kill those also that came for water to quench the fire. Whilst these plans were preparing, it happened there were two ambassadors from **the Allobroges** staying in Rome; a nation at that time in a distressed condition, and very uneasy under the Roman government. These Lentulus (#1) and his party judging useful instruments to move and seduce **Gaul** to revolt, admitted into the conspiracy, and they gave them letters to their own magistrates, and letters to Catiline; in the first they promised liberty, in the others they exhorted Catiline to set all slaves free, and to bring them along with him to Rome. They sent also to accompany them to Catiline, one Titus, a native of Croton, who was to carry those letters to him.

[These attempts to involve the ambassadors] *[omission]* were easily found out by Cicero: who had a careful eye upon [the conspirators], and very wisely and discreetly saw through them. For he had appointed men out of the city to spy their doings, which followed them to see what they intended. Furthermore he spoke secretly with some he trusted (the which others also took to be of the conspiracy) and knew by them that Lentulus and Cethegus had practised with the ambassadors of the Allobroges, and drawn them into their conspiracy. At length he watched them one night so narrowly, that he took the ambassadors, and Titus Crotonian with the letters he carried, by help of the ambassadors of the Allobroges, which had secretly informed him of all before.

The next morning by break of day, Cicero assembled the Senate in the **Temple of Concord**, and there openly read the letters, and heard the evidence of the witnesses. Further, there was one Junius Silanus, a senator that gave in evidence, that some heard Cethegus say they should kill three consuls, and four praetors. Pisa, a senator also, and that had been consul, told in manner the selfsame tale. And Gaius Sulpitius, a praetor, that was sent into Cethegus' house, reported that he had found great store of darts, armour, daggers and swords new made. Lastly [came Titus Crotonian], the Senate having promised [him] he should have no hurt, if he would tell what he knew of this conspiracy.

Lentulus thereby was convicted, and driven to give up his office of praetor before the Senate, and changing his purple gown, to take another meet for his miserable state. This being done, Lentulus and his **consorts** were taken to the praetors' houses, and put in their custody.

Part Two

Now growing towards evening, the people waiting about the place where the Senate was assembled, Cicero at length came out, and told them what they had done within. Thereupon he was conveyed by all the people unto the house of a friend and near neighbour; for his own house was occupied by the women, who were celebrating with secret rites **the feast of the goddess whom the Romans call the Good**, and the Greeks the Women's goddess. For a sacrifice is annually performed to her in the consul's house, either by his wife or mother, in the presence of the Vestal Nuns.

Now Cicero being come into his neighbour's house, began to bethink him what course he were best to take in this matter. For, to punish the offenders with severity, according to **their deserts**, he was afraid to do it: both because he was of a courteous nature, as also for that he would not seem to be glad to have occasion to show his absolute power and authority, to punish (as he might) with rigour, citizens that were of the noblest houses of the city, and that had besides many friends. And contrariwise also, being remiss in so weighty a matter as this, he was afraid of the danger that might ensue of their rashness, mistrusting that if he should punish them with less than death, they would not **amend** for it, imagining they were well rid of their trouble, but would rather become more bold and desperate than ever they were: adding moreover the sting and spite of a new malice unto their accustomed wickedness; besides that he himself should be thought a coward and a **timorous** man, whereas they had already not much better opinion of him.

Cicero being perplexed thus with these doubts, there appeared a miracle to the ladies doing sacrifice in his house. For on the altar, where the fire seemed wholly extinguished, a great and bright flame issued forth from the ashes of the burnt wood; at which others were affrighted. Howbeit the Vestal Nuns willed Terentia (Cicero's wife) to go straight unto her husband, and to bid him not to be afraid to execute that boldly which he had considered of, for the benefit of his country; and that the goddess had raised this great flame to show him that he should have great honour by doing of it.

Terentia, therefore, as she was otherwise in her own nature neither tender-hearted nor timorous, but a woman eager for distinction (who, as Cicero himself says, would rather thrust herself into his public affairs than communicate her domestic matters to him), told him these things, and excited him against the conspirators. The like did Quintus Cicero his brother, and also Publius Nigidius, one of his philosophical friends, whom he often made use of in his greatest and most weighty affairs of state.

Part Three

The next day, a debate arising in the Senate about the punishment of the men, Silanus, being the first who was asked his opinion, said it was fit they should be all sent to the prison, and from thence to suffer execution. Others likewise that followed him, were all of that mind, except for **Gaius Caesar,** that afterwards came to be dictator. He was then but a young man, and only at the outset of his career, but had already directed his hopes and policy to that course by which he afterwards changed the Roman state into a monarchy. For at that time, Cicero had vehement suspicions of Caesar, but no apparent proof to convince him. And some say, that it was brought so near, as he was almost convicted, but yet saved himself. Others write to the contrary, that Cicero wittingly **dissembled** that he either heard or knew any signs which were told him against Caesar, being afraid indeed of his friends and power; for it was very evident to everybody that if Caesar was to be accused with the conspirators, they were more likely to be saved with him, than he to be punished with them.

Now when Caesar came to deliver his opinion touching the

punishment of these prisoners: he stood up and said that he did not think it good to put them to death, but to confiscate their goods: and as for their persons, that they should bestow them in prison, some in one place, some in another, in such cities of Italy, as pleased Cicero best, until the war of Catiline were ended. This sentence being very mild, and the author thereof marvellous eloquent to make it good: Cicero himself gave no small weight, for he stood up and, turning the scale on either side, spoke in favour partly of the former, partly of Caesar's sentence.

His friends thinking that Caesar's opinion was the safest for Cicero, because thereby he should deserve less blame for that he had not put the prisoners to death: they followed rather the second. Whereupon Sullanus also recanted that which he had spoken, and expounded his opinion: saying, that when he spoke they should be put to death, he meant nothing so, but thought the last punishment a senator of Rome could have was the prison.

But the first that contraried this opinion, was Catulus Lutatius, and after him **Cato**, who with vehement words enforced the suspicion of Caesar, and furthermore filled all the Senate with wrath and courage: so that even upon the instant it was decreed by most voices, that they should suffer death. But Caesar opposed the confiscation of their goods, not thinking it fair that those who rejected the mildest part of his sentence should avail themselves of the severest. And when many insisted upon it, he appealed to the tribunes, but they would do nothing; till Cicero himself yielding, remitted that part of the sentence.

Narration and Discussion

Why was Caesar's recommendation of punishment fairly mild, and why were the Senators inclined to agree with him? What changed their minds?

Did Cicero make the right choice? Did he even have a choice?

Creative narration #1: Part Three could be written as a newspaper account, or acted out with a group of students.

Creative narration #2 (for older students): Plutarch says that Cicero discussed his decision with his brother Titus Quintus Cicero, and also with a senator named Publius Nigidius Figulus, both of whom agreed that the conspirators should be put to death. Imagine that another friend takes the opposite view. What arguments might be made?

Lesson Six

Introduction

Cicero handled the aftermath of the conspiracy as calmly as he could. His courage to act had saved the city from destruction. However, his enemies were eager to turn a reason for praise into the chance to destroy him.

Vocabulary

inauspicious: unlucky

forsook him: left him alone, disappeared

some few days before Cicero's consulate expired: Some of the Roman magistracies followed a different election schedule.

usurpation: unlawfully seizing power or position

though he was intemperately fond of his own glory: North says "though he had this worm of ambition"

covetous: envious; having a great desire for wealth or power

forgetting the many high encomiums he continually passes upon him: ignoring the frequent praise he gives to him

Philippics: see note under **People**. Plutarch is looking ahead here; there will be more about Cicero's "Philippics" in **Lesson Eleven**.

People

Antonius (#1): Gaius Antonius Hybrida, consul with Cicero in 63 B.C.

Mark Antony (or **Marc Antony, or Marcus Antonius (#2))**: Roman politician and general, who would be part of the Second Triumvirate.

Demosthenes: A famous Athenian orator, known for his speeches against Philip of Macedon, called the **Philippics**.

Historic Occasions

December 63 B.C.: Execution of Lentulus and other conspirators

January 62 B.C.: Catiline killed at the Battle of Pistoria

Reading

Part One

Cicero went with the Senate to fetch the prisoners: who were not all in one house, but every praetor had one of them. So he went first to take Lentulus (#1) from the Palatine, and brought him through the Sacred Street and the marketplace, accompanied with the chiefest men of the city, who compassed him round about, and guarded his person. The people seeing that, quaked and trembled with fear, passed by, and said never a word: and specially the young men, as if, with fear and trembling, they were undergoing a rite of initiation into some ancient sacred mysteries of aristocratic power.

So when he had passed through the marketplace, and was come to the prison, he delivered Lentulus into the hands of the hangman, and commanded him to do execution. Afterwards also Cethegus, and then all the rest one after another, whom he brought to the prison himself, and caused them to be executed. Furthermore, seeing many of the conspirators in a troop together in the marketplace, who knew nothing of what he had done, and watched only till night were come, supposing then to take away their companions by force from the place where they were, thinking they were yet alive: he called out in a loud voice, and said, "They did live"; for so the Romans, to avoid **inauspicious** language, name those that are dead.

When night was come, and that he was going homeward, as he came through the marketplace, the people did wait upon him no more with silence as before, but with great cries of his praise, and clapping of hands in every place he went; they called him "saviour," and "second founder of Rome." Besides all this, at every man's door there were torches lighted, so that it was as light in the streets as at noonday. The very women also did put lights out of the tops of their houses to do him honour, and also to see him so nobly brought home, with such a long train of the chiefest men of the city.

They said that the Romans were greatly bound to many captains and generals of armies in their time, for the wonderful riches, spoils, and increase of their power which they had won: howbeit that they were to thank Cicero only for their health and preservation, having saved them from so great and extreme a danger. For though it might seem no wonderful thing to prevent the design, and punish the conspirators, yet to defeat the greatest of all conspiracies with so little disturbance, trouble, and commotion, was very extraordinary. For the most part of them that were gathered together about Catiline, when they heard that Lentulus and all the rest were put to death, they presently **forsook him**: and Catiline himself, with his remaining forces, joining battle with **Antonius (#1)**, was destroyed with his army.

Part Two

And yet there were some who were very ready both to speak ill of Cicero, and to do him hurt for these actions; and they had for their leaders some of the magistrates of the coming year, such as Caesar, who was one of the praetors, and Metellus and Bestia, the tribunes. These, entering upon their office **some few days before Cicero's consulate expired**, would not permit him to make any address to the people, but throwing the benches before the speaker's platform, hindered his speaking, telling him he might, if he pleased, make the oath of withdrawal from office, and then come down again. Cicero, accordingly, accepting the conditions, came forward to make his withdrawal; and silence being made, he recited his oath, not in the usual, but in a new and peculiar form, namely, that he had saved his country and preserved the empire; the truth of which oath all the people confirmed with theirs. Caesar and the tribunes, all the more exasperated by this, endeavoured to create him further trouble, and for this purpose proposed a law for calling Pompey home with his army, to put an end to Cicero's "**usurpation**."

But it was a very great advantage for Cicero and the whole commonwealth that Cato was at that time one of the tribunes. For he, being of equal power with the rest, and of greater reputation, could oppose their designs. He easily defeated their other projects, and in an oration to the people so highly extolled Cicero's consulate, that the greatest honours were decreed him, and he was publicly declared the "Father of the Country," which title he seems to have obtained, the first man who did so, when Cato gave it to him in this address to the people.

At this time, therefore, his authority was very great in the city; but he created himself much envy, and offended very many, not by any evil action, but only because he too did too much boast of himself. For he never was in any assembly of people, Senate, or judgement, but every man's head was full still to hear the sound of Catulus and Lentulus (#1) brought in for sport, and filling the books and works he compiled besides full of his own praises: the which made his sweet and pleasant style tedious, and troublesome to those that heard them, as though this misfortune ever followed him to take away his excellent grace.

Nevertheless, **though he was intemperately fond of his own glory**, he was very free from envying others, and was, on the contrary, most liberally profuse in commending both the ancients and his contemporaries, as anyone may see in his writings. And many such sayings of his are also remembered; as that he called Aristotle a river of flowing gold; and said of Plato's dialogues, that if Jupiter were to speak, it would be in language like theirs. Of Theophrastus, he was wont to call him his delight; and of **Demosthenes'** orations, when one asked him on a time which of them he liked best: "The longest," said he.

And yet some affected imitators of Demosthenes have complained of some words that occur in one of his letters, to the effect that Demosthenes sometimes falls asleep in his speeches; **forgetting the many high encomiums he continually passes upon him**, and the compliment he paid him when he named the most elaborate of all his own orations, those he wrote against **Mark Antony**, the "**Philippics**."

[omission for length]

Narration and Discussion

Although Cicero was officially named "Father of the Country," how did he manage to make himself unpopular?

On the other hand, how did he show magnanimity? (One definition of magnanimity is to show a generous spirit.)

Creative narration: Write or act out the following scene: Cicero is rehearsing a speech, and one of his other **Old School Friends** gives him some honest feedback. Cicero, however, does not seem to see the problem.

Lesson Seven

Introduction

This lesson begins with examples of Cicero's wit and sarcasm, which, as Plutarch points out, could turn bitter and nasty.

The rest of the lesson is a story which appears also in the *Life of Julius Caesar*: the adventures of Publius Clodius Pulcher, who crashed a females-only religious ceremony at Caesar's house.

Vocabulary

invectives: insults, abuse

fine taunts and girds: cutting humour, mean jokes

insolent: rude, disrespectful

put her away: divorced her

People

Vatinius: Publius Vatinius, a politician who, having been given a position in Puteoli which involved receiving money from the local people, carried out his duties with a little too much enthusiasm.

Clodius: Publius Clodius Pulcher, a Roman politician who was considered to be an **agitator**, or one who stirs things up.

Historic Occasions

62 B.C.: Clodius disrupts a ceremony at Caesar's house

60 B.C.: Julius Caesar invited Cicero to partner with himself, Pompey and Crassus in the **First Triumvirate**; but Cicero declined the offer

59 B.C.: The year that Julius Caesar was consul, referred to jestingly as "the consulship of Julius and Caesar."

On the Map

Syria: This province was another recent acquisition for Rome.

Reading

Part One

[We omit some of Cicero's witticisms as not being fit for young ears. However, a few of his milder ones follow]

When Crassus was about to go into **Syria**, he desired to leave Cicero rather his friend than his enemy, and, therefore, one day saluting him, told him he would come and sup with him, which the other as courteously received. Within a few days after, on some of Cicero's acquaintances interceding for **Vatinius**, as desirous of reconciliation and friendship, for he was then his enemy, "What," Cicero replied, "does Vatinius also wish to come and sup with me?" When Vatinius, who had swellings in his neck, was pleading a cause, he called him "the swollen orator." Having been told by someone that Vatinius was dead, (and then) hearing that he was alive, "May the rascal perish," said he, "for his news not being true."

To a young man who was suspected of having given a poisoned cake to his father, and who talked largely of the **invectives** he meant to deliver against Cicero, "Better these," replied he, "than your cakes."

Lucius Cotta, a lover of wine, was censor when Cicero stood for the consulship. Cicero, being thirsty at the election, his friends stood round about him while he was drinking. "You have reason to be afraid," he said, "lest the censor should be angry with me for drinking water."

When Marcus Appius, in the opening of some speech in a court of justice, said that his friend had desired him to employ industry, eloquence, and fidelity in that cause, Cicero answered, "And how have you had the heart not to accede to any one of his requests?"

Now to use **fine taunts and girds** to his enemies, it was a part of a good orator: but so commonly to gird every man to make the people laugh, that won him great ill-will of many.

Part Two

The great ill-will that **Clodius** bare him began upon this occasion. Clodius was of a noble house, a young man, and very wild and **insolent**. He being in love with Pompeia, Caesar's wife, found the means secretly to get into Caesar's house, in the dress and attire of a music-girl, because on that day the ladies of Rome did solemnly celebrate a secret sacrifice in Caesar's house, which is not lawful for men to be present at. So there was no man there but Clodius, who thought he should not have been known, because he was but a young man without any hair on his face, and that by this means he might come to Pompeia amongst the other women. He being gotten into this great house by night, not knowing the rooms and chambers in it: there was one of Caesar's mother's maids of her chamber called Aurelia, who seeing him wandering up and down the house in this sort, asked him what he was, and how they called him. So being forced to answer, he said he sought for Aura, one of Pompeia's maids. The maid perceived straight it was no woman's voice, and therewithal gave a great shriek, and called the other women: the which did see the gates fast shut, and then sought every corner up and down, so that at length they found him in the maid's chamber, with whom he came in. This matter being much talked about, Caesar **put away his wife**, Pompeia, and Clodius was prosecuted for profaning the holy rites.

Cicero was at that time [Clodius's] friend, for he had been useful to him in the conspiracy of Catiline, as one of his assistants and protectors. But when Clodius rested his defense upon this point, that he was not then at Rome, but at a distance in the country, Cicero testified that he had come to his house that day, and conversed with him on several matters; which thing was indeed true, although Cicero was thought to testify it not so much for the truth's sake, as to please his wife Terentia: for she [had a personal grudge against Clodius], and urged him on to taking a part against Clodius, and delivering his testimony.

[Necessary omission: some of the evils that Clodius was said to have committed]

Notwithstanding all this, when the common people united against the accusers and witnesses and the whole party, the judges were affrighted, and a guard was placed about them the judges for their defense; and most of them wrote their sentences on the tablets in such a way that they could not well be read. It was decided, however, that there was a majority for his acquittal, and bribery was reported to have been employed *[omission for length]*. Notwithstanding, in this judgement Caesar never gave evidence against Clodius: and said moreover, that he did not think his wife had committed any adultery, howbeit that he had **put her away**, because he would that Caesar's wife should not only be clean from any dishonesty, but also void of all suspicion.

Narration and Discussion

Do you enjoy Cicero's sense of humour, or not? How would you feel if you were on the receiving end?

Why didn't Caesar give evidence against Clodius?

For further thought: Is it better to be eloquent, or to be truthful? Can you be both?

Creative narration: Interview someone who was in Caesar's house during the Clodius incident, such as the maid, or one of the women.

Note: Some students may want to act out the story of Clodius sneaking around in Caesar's house, and it does have its lighter moments. However, it must be kept in mind that the Roman women were not having a party, but carrying out a sacred rite, so what Clodius did (apart from his attempt to visit Caesar's wife) was viewed as a religious offense. There is also the fact that Clodius was not just a foolish youth acting on a dare: he was over thirty years old, and, although he had helped defend Rome against Catiline, he was not at all a person of good morals. Perhaps this story should be remembered more for its consequences than for its comedy.

Lesson Eight

Introduction

After his acquittal, Clodius pursued every bit of power he could. As a tribune, he made himself popular by proposing laws that favoured everyone from the consuls to the common people. Then he played his best card: accusing Cicero of wrongfully executing the leaders of the Catiline Conspiracy.

Vocabulary

tribune: a Roman official concerned with matters of justice to the common people (see introductory notes)

the three men then in power: Julius Caesar, Pompey, and Crassus; also called the **First Triumvirate**

indifferently made advances to both: Pompey made offers of friendship to both Crassus and Cicero, but was not especially loyal to either of them

made fair weather with him: treated him in a friendly manner

he gave up his lieutenancy unto Caesar: As Plutarch explains, Cicero had applied to go with Caesar into Gaul. His proposed absence from Rome did not please Clodius, who had just been chosen tribune and was looking forward to his opportunity to get all kinds of revenge.

to plead as he did before: went back to his public business

sued to the people; supplicating: begging their understanding and mercy

determine it by the sword: fight it out

Pompey being now Caesar's son-in-law: In 59 B.C., Pompey married Caesar's daughter Julia.

tarry: stay where he was

tumult and sedition: a state of unrest, rebellion

Minerva: the Roman goddess of wisdom and justice, similar to the Greek goddess Athena. She is represented by an owl.

caused bills of inhibition to be set up: passed an act forbidding people to shelter or aid Cicero.

fainthearted: frightened, cowardly

used him: treated him

tinctures: this usually refers to medicines, but can also refer to residue, faint tinges or traces of something

People

Gabinius, Piso (#1): consuls for 58 B.C.

Piso (#2): see introductory notes

Historic Occasions

58 B.C.: Cicero went into exile.

On the Map

Lucania: a region of southern Italy

Brundisium: a city in **Apulia**, on the Adriatic Sea, now called Brindisi

Dyrrhachium (Dyrrachium): a city on the Adriatic Sea, now called Durrës, in present-day Albania

Reading

Part One

Clodius, having escaped this danger, and having got himself chosen one of the **tribunes**, immediately attacked Cicero, heaping up all matters and inciting all persons against him. The common people he gained over with popular laws; to each of the consuls he decreed large provinces: to **Piso** (#1), Macedonia, and to **Gabinius**, Syria. He made many poor men free citizens, and had always about him a great number of slaves, armed.

Of **the three men then in power**, Crassus was Cicero's open enemy, Pompey **indifferently made advances to both**, and Caesar was going with an army into Gaul. To him, though not his friend (what had occurred in the time of the conspiracy having created suspicions between them), Cicero applied, requesting an appointment as one of his lieutenants in the province. Caesar accepted him, and Clodius, perceiving that by this means he (Cicero) got himself out of the danger of his (Clodius') office of tribuneship for that year, he **made fair weather with him** (as though he meant to reconcile himself unto him), and laid the greatest fault upon Terentia, made always a favourable mention of him, and addressed him with kind expressions, as one who felt no hatred or ill-will, but who merely wished to urge his complaints in a moderate and friendly way.

These sweet words made Cicero no more afraid**,** so that **he gave up his lieutenancy unto Caesar**, and began again **to plead as he did before**. At which Caesar, being exasperated, joined the party of Clodius against him, and wholly alienated Pompey from him. And Caesar himself also said, before all the people, that he thought Cicero had put Lentulus (#1), Cethegus, and the rest unjustly to death, and contrary to law, without lawful trial and condemnation. And this was the fault for the which Cicero was openly accused. And so, as an accused man, and in danger for the result, he changed his dress, and put on a mourning gown: and so suffering his beard and hair of his head to grow without any combing, he went in this humble manner, and **sued to the people**. But Clodius was ever about him in every place and street he went, having a band of rascals and knaves with him that shamefully mocked him Cicero for that he had changed his gown and countenance in that sort, and oftentimes they cast dirt and stones at him, breaking his talk and requests he made unto the people.

This notwithstanding, almost the whole equestrian order changed their dress with him, and of them there were commonly twenty thousand young gentlemen of noble house which followed him, with their hair also untrimmed, and **supplicating** with him to the people. Furthermore, the Senate assembled to decree that the people should mourn in blacks, as in a common calamity; but the consuls were against it. And Clodius, on the other side, was with a band of armed men about the Senate, so that many of the senators ran out of the Senate, crying and tearing their clothes for sorrow. But this sight moved neither shame nor pity: Cicero must either fly, or **determine it by the sword** with Clodius.

Part Two

Then went Cicero to entreat Pompey to aid him: but he (Pompey) absented himself of purpose out of the city, because he would not be entreated, and lay at one of his houses in the country, near unto the city of Alba; and first he sent his son-in-law **Piso (#2)** to intercede with him, and afterwards set out to go himself. Of which Pompey being informed, would not stay to look him in the face: for he had been past all shame to have refused the request of so worthy a man, who had before shown him such pleasure, and also done and said so many things in his favour. But **Pompey being now Caesar's son-in-law**, at his instance he had set aside all former kindness, and, slipping out at another door, avoided the interview.

So Cicero seeing himself betrayed of him, and now having no other refuge to whom he might repair unto: he put himself into the hands of the two consuls. Gabinius was rough with him, as usual; but Piso (#1) spoke more courteously, desiring him to yield and give place for a little while to Clodius' fury, and patiently to bear the change of the time: for in so doing, he might come again another time to be the preserver of his country, which was now for his sake in **tumult and sedition**.

Cicero, receiving this answer, consulted with his friends. Lucullus advised him to stay, as being sure to prevail at last; others [counselled him] to flee, because the people would soon desire him again, when they had once been beaten with Clodius' fury and folly. Cicero liked best to follow this counsel. But first he took a statue of **Minerva**, which had been long set up and greatly honoured in his house, and carrying it to the Capitol, there dedicated it, with the inscription, "To Minerva, Patroness of Rome.") And receiving an escort from his friends, about the middle of the night he left the city, and went by land through **Lucania**, intending to reach Sicily.

Part Three

When it was known in Rome that he was fled, Clodius did presently banish him by decree of the people, and **caused bills of inhibition to be set up**, that no man should secretly receive him within five hundred miles' compass of Italy. Most people, out of respect for Cicero, paid no regard to this edict, offering him every attention, and escorting him on his way. But at Hipponium (a city of Lucania now called Vibo), one Vibius, a Sicilian by birth, who, amongst many other instances of Cicero's friendships had been made head of the state engineers when he was consul, would not receive him into his house, but promised him he would appoint him a place in the country that he might go unto. And Gaius Vergilius also, at that time praetor and governor of Sicily, who before had shown himself his very great friend, wrote then unto him, that he should not come near unto Sicily.

At these things Cicero, being disheartened, went to **Brundisium**, whence putting forth with a prosperous wind, a contrary gale blowing from the sea carried him back to Italy the next day. He put again to sea, and having reached **Dyrrhachium**, on his coming to shore there, it is reported that an earthquake and a convulsion in the sea happened at the same time, signs whereby the soothsayers interpreted that his exile should not be long, because both the one and the other was a token of change.

Yet Cicero, notwithstanding that many men came to see him for the goodwill they bore him, and that the cities of Greece contended who should most honour him, he was always sad, and could not be merry, but cast his eyes still towards Italy, as passioned lovers do towards the women they love: showing himself **fainthearted**, and took this adversity more basely than was looked for of one so well studied and learned as he. And yet he oftentimes prayed his friends, not to call him orator, but rather philosopher, because he had made philosophy his business, and had only used rhetoric as an instrument for attaining his objects in public life. . But the desire of glory has great power in washing the **tinctures** of philosophy out of the souls of men, and in imprinting the passions of the common people, by custom and conversation, in the minds of those that take a part in governing them, unless the politician be very careful so to engage in public affairs as to interest himself only in the affairs themselves, but not participate in the passions that are consequent to them.

Narration and Discussion

How did Clodius win the favour of the people as tribune?

Why did Pompey refuse to help Cicero when he was in trouble?

Plutarch says that the few friends that Cicero had left (possibly including his **Old School Friends**) gave him conflicting advice about how to handle his sudden unpopularity. What was Lucullus' reasoning on it? What would you have done?

Creative narration: When Cicero was exiled, "…he was always sad, and could not be merry…showing himself fainthearted, and took this adversity more basely than was looked for of one so well studied and learned as he." Do you agree that Cicero, being a "philosopher at heart," might have shown a bit more stamina? Write or act out a conversation, or write a letter from a friend, discussing this point.

Lesson Nine

Introduction

Cicero's power struggle with Clodius continued for five years after he returned from exile, and ended only with the death of Clodius (by the orders of a political enemy). Surprisingly, this gave Cicero a "reboot" on his political career, and he was appointed as governor in Cilicia.

But his return to Rome in 50 B.C. marked the end of an era, and not only for himself: the Republic was about to be rocked by change.

Vocabulary

exposed to sale by daily proclamation: put up for auction

overthrown and razed: destroyed

took away the tables, and broke them: (Dryden says he "tore and defaced" them.) Cicero destroyed the public record of Clodius's acts as tribune, saying that those acts were illegal, since Clodius should technically not have been allowed to even be a tribune. Tribunes were supposed to be elected from the common people, although occasionally there were exceptions.

Cato was offended: This story is also told in the *Life of Cato the Younger.*

six hundred: North says five hundred

not sumptuously but liberally: generously, but not to excess

porter: a servant in charge of the entrance

rent: torn

reviled: attacked, condemned

many things: Dryden refers to money, rather than other stolen goods

Imperator, **that is to say, "chief captain":** The term *Imperator* is sometimes translated "emperor," but in this context it is more like "great commander."

People

Lentulus (#2): Publius Cornelius Lentulus Spinther, the consul for 57 B.C. (not to be confused with Lentulus the conspirator)

Publius: Publius Licinius Crassus (86 or 82 B.C.-53 B.C.), son of Marcus Licinius Crassus. It shows something of his character that he was a friend and loyal supporter of Cicero, since Cicero and his father were often not on good terms. Cicero seems to have admired Publius in return, although not so much his military ambitions).

Historic Occasions

57 B.C.: Cicero returned from exile

53 B.C.: Deaths of Crassus and his son Publius (in battle against the Parthians)

52 B.C.: Death of Clodius

51-50 B.C.: Cicero was governor in Cilicia

On the Map

Cyprus: the third-largest island in the Mediterranean Sea. It was annexed by the Romans in 58 B.C.

Byzantium: the ancient city later known as Constantinople/Istanbul

Parthia (Parthians): a region which is part of present-day Iran

Cilicia, Cappadocia: regions of present-day Turkey, which had become Roman provinces. **Cilicia**, at that time, included the island of **Cyprus**.

Caria: a region of western **Anatolia**, part of present-day Turkey

Reading

Part One

Clodius, having thus driven away Cicero, fell to burning his farms and villas, and afterwards his city house; and built on the site of it a temple to Liberty. The rest of Cicero's property he **exposed to sale by daily proclamation**, but nobody came to buy. The chiefest men of the city beginning to be afraid of these violent parts, and having the common people at his commandment, whom he had made very bold and insolent: he began to inveigh against Pompey, and spoke ill of his doings in the time of his wars, the which every man else but himself did commend. Pompey; then was very angry with himself that he had so forsaken Cicero, and repented him of it; and by his friends procured all the means he could to call him home again from his banishment. And when Clodius opposed it, the Senate made vote that no public measure should be ratified or passed by them till Cicero was recalled. But when **Lentulus (#2)** was consul, the commotions grew so high upon this matter, that the tribunes were wounded in the Forum, and Quintus, Cicero's brother, was left as dead, lying unobserved amongst the slain.

Then the people began to change their minds. And Titus Annius Milo, one of the tribunes, was the first who took confidence to summon Clodius to trial for acts of violence. Pompey himself also having gotten a great number of men about him, as well of the city of Rome as of other towns adjoining to it, being strongly guarded with them: he came out of his house, and compelled Clodius to get him out of the Forum, and then called the people to give their voices for the calling home again of Cicero. It is reported that the people never passed a thing with so great goodwill, nor so wholly together, as the return of Cicero. And the Senate for their parts also, in the behalf of Cicero, ordained that the cities which had honoured and received Cicero in his exile, should be greatly commended: and that his houses which Clodius had **overthrown and razed**, should be rebuilt at the charge of the commonwealth.

So Cicero returned in the sixteenth month after his banishment, and the towns and cities he came by, showed themselves so joyful of his return, that all manner of men went to meet and honour him, with so great love and affection, that Cicero's report thereof afterwards came indeed short of the very truth as it was. For he said, that Italy brought him into Rome upon their shoulders. And Crassus himself, who had been his enemy before his exile, went then voluntarily to meet him, and was reconciled, to please his son **Publius**, as he said, who was Cicero's affectionate admirer.

Part Two

Now Cicero being returned, he found a time when Clodius was out of the city, and went with a good company of his friends unto the Capitol, and there **took away the tables, and broke them**, in the which Clodius had written all his acts that he had passed and done in the time of his tribuneship. Clodius would afterwards have accused Cicero for it: but Cicero answered him, that he was not lawfully created tribune, because he was of the patricians, and therefore nothing done by him was valid. Therewith **Cato was offended**, and spoke against him, not for that he liked any of Clodius' doings: (but to the contrary, utterly misliked all that he did), but because he thought it out of all reason that the Senate should cancel all those things which he had done and passed in his tribuneship, and specially, because amongst the rest that was there which he himself had done in the isle of **Cyprus**, and in the city of **Byzantium**. Hereupon there grew some strangeness betwixt Cicero and Cato, which, though it came not to open enmity, yet made a more reserved friendship between them.

[omitted for length: Titus Annius Milo's killing of Clodius]

Part Three

Cicero was made one of the priests, whom the Romans call *augurs*, in place of Crassus the Younger, who was dead in **Parthia**. Then he was appointed by lot to the province of **Cilicia**, and set sail thither with twelve thousand foot soldiers, and two thousand **six hundred** horse. He had orders to bring back **Cappadocia** to its allegiance to Ariobarzanes, its king; which settlement he effected very completely without recourse to arms. And perceiving the Cilicians, by the great loss the Romans had suffered in Parthia, and the commotions in Syria, to have become disposed to attempt a revolt, by a gentle course of government he soothed them back into fidelity.

He would accept none of the presents that were offered him by the kings. Furthermore, he did disburden the provinces of the feasts and banquets they were wont to make other governors before him. On the other side also, he would ever have the company of good and learned men at his table, and would treat them well, **not sumptuously but liberally**. His house had no **porter**, nor was he seen by any man in his bed: for he would always rise at the break of day, and would walk or stand before his door. He would courteously receive all them that came to salute and visit him. Further, they report of him that he never caused any of those under his command to be beaten with rods, or to have their garments **rent**. In his anger he never **reviled** any man, neither did despitefully set a fine upon any man's head.

Finding **many things** also belonging to the commonwealth, which private men had stolen and embezzled to their own use: he restored them again unto the cities, whereby they grew very rich and wealthy: and yet did he save their honour and credit that had taken them away, and did them no other hurt, but only constrained them to restore that which was the commonwealth's. He made a little war also, and drove away the thieves that kept about Mount Amanus, for the which exploit his soldiers called him *Imperator,* **that is to say, "chief captain."**

To Caecilius the orator, who asked him to send him some panthers from Cilicia, to be exhibited in the theater at Rome, he wrote, in commendation of his own actions, that there were no panthers in Cilicia, for they were all fled to **Caria**, in anger that, seeing all things quiet in Cilicia, the Cilicians had leisure now to hunt them.

Narration and Discussion

"It is reported that the people never passed a thing with so great goodwill, nor so wholly together, as the return of Cicero." Tell the story of his homecoming.

Creative narration #1: Interview someone living in Cilicia at that time, and ask their opinion of Governor Cicero.

Creative narration #2 (for older students): Did you find it surprising that, at this time of his life, Cicero "made a little war also," and, apparently, did it so well that he was called *Imperator?* Write a letter from one of the **Old School Friends** to another, sharing this news.

Lesson Ten

Introduction

When Cicero returned from Cilicia, he found Rome on the brink of civil war. Which side should he take, Caesar's or Pompey's? Maybe, he thought, he could convince them to settle their differences.

A great deal of history happens in this lesson and in those that follow. To make things very short, Julius Caesar came into Rome, and Pompey went out (and was killed in battle soon afterwards). Cicero, having joined Pompey's camp, was given a pardon by Caesar; however, he felt it prudent at that time to retire from his public life.

How old was Cicero?

The question of Cicero's advanced age was raised in a rather rude letter suggesting that he might want to get himself somewhere safe during the war. He would have been about fifty-seven in 49 B.C. Pompey was the same age, and Julius Caesar was six years younger.

Vocabulary

in a flame, breaking out into a civil war: see note under **Historic Occasions**

decreed him a triumph: Military heroes were given an official parade through Rome, called a triumph.

epistles: letters

reproved: scolded, criticized

depreciating Pompey's resources: scoffing at how poorly outfitted and prepared Pompey's army seemed to be

Battle of Pharsalus (Pharsalia): see note under **Historic Occasions**

tarried: lingered, stayed

he was driven against his will to set Ligarius at liberty: Caesar's pardoning of Ligarius allowed him to return to Rome, but Ligarius continued his hatred of Caesar and became involved in the plot to assassinate him.

kingdom: under the rule of one person

Cicero leaving to practice…: he ended his public activities

all the Greek words which are proper unto logic and natural causes: philosophical and scientific terms

he exercised his dexterity: he kept his skills and his mind occupied

"the life of Laertes": a life of ease

People

the younger Pompey: one of the two sons of Pompey

Pericles and Theramenes: famous Athenian statesmen

Quintus Ligarius: a Roman general, one of the conspirators against Julius Caesar

Historic Occasions

January, 49 B.C.: Caesar crossed the Rubicon into Italy, an act of defiance which began a civil war

February, 49 B.C.: Pompey fled to Greece along with most of the Senate

August 48 B.C.: Battle of Pharsalus, in which Caesar defeated Pompey (and Pompey died soon afterwards)

On the Map

Tarentum: a city in **Apulia**

Tusculum: a city in the **Latium** region of Italy

Reading

Part One

On leaving his province, he came by Rhodes: and stayed a few days at Athens, with great delight, to remember how pleasantly he lived there before, at what time he studied there. Thither came to him the chiefest learned men of the city, and his friends also, with whom he was acquainted at his first being there; and after receiving in Greece the honours that were due to him, returned to Rome, where everything was now just as it were **in a flame, breaking out into a civil war**.

When the Senate would have **decreed him a triumph**, he told them he had rather, so differences were accommodated, follow the triumphal chariot of Caesar. In private, he gave advice to both Caesar and Pompey, writing many letters to Caesar, and personally entreating Pompey; doing his best to soothe and bring to reason both the one and the other. But when matters became incurable, and Caesar was approaching Rome, Pompey dared not abide it, but, with many honest citizens, left the city. Cicero would not follow him when he fled, and therefore men thought he would take part with Caesar; but this is certain, that he was in a marvellous perplexity, and could not easily determine what way to take.

Whereupon he wrote in his **epistles**:

> "To which side should I turn? Pompey has the fair
> and honourable plea for war; and Caesar, on the
> other hand, has managed his affairs better, and is
> more able to secure himself and his friends. So that
> I know whom I should fly (from), not whom I
> should fly to."

But when Trebatius, one of Caesar's friends, by letter signified to him that Caesar thought it was his most desirable course to join his party, and partake his hopes, but if he considered himself too old a man for this, then he should retire into Greece, and stay quietly there, out of the way of either party; Cicero, wondering that Caesar had not written himself, gave an angry reply, that he should not do anything unbecoming his past life. Such is the account to be collected from his letters.

Part Two

Now Caesar being gone into Spain, Cicero embarked immediately to go to Pompey. So when he came unto him, every man was very glad of his coming, but Cato. Howbeit Cato secretly **reproved** him for coming unto Pompey. As for himself, he said, it had been indecent to forsake that part in the commonwealth which he had chosen from the beginning; but Cicero might have been more useful to his country and friends, if, remaining neutral, he had attended and used his influence to moderate the result, instead of coming hither to make himself, without reason or necessity, an enemy to Caesar, and a partner in such great dangers.

These persuasions of Cato overthrew all Cicero's purpose and determination, besides that Pompey himself did not employ him in any matter of service or importance. Although, indeed, he was himself the cause of it, by his not denying that he was sorry he had come, by his **depreciating Pompey's resources**, finding fault underhand with his counsels, and continually indulging in jests and sarcastic remarks on his fellow-soldiers. Though he went about in the camp with a gloomy and melancholy face himself, he was always trying to raise a laugh in others, whether they wished it or not.

[omission: Cicero's jokes, because you really had to be there]

Part Three

After the **Battle of Pharsalia**, where Cicero was not present for want of health: Pompey being fled, and Cato at that time at Dyrrhachium, where he had gathered a great number of men of war, and had also prepared a great navy: he would have had Cicero commander-in-chief, according to law and the precedence of his consular dignity. And on his refusing the command, and wholly declining to take part in their plans for continuing the war, he was in the greatest danger of being killed, **the younger Pompey** and his friends called him traitor, and drew their swords upon him to kill him, which they would had done, had not Cato stepped between them and him; and yet had he (Cato) much ado to save him, and to convey him safely out of the camp.

Afterwards, arriving at Brundisium, he **tarried** there some time in expectation of Caesar, who was delayed by his affairs in Asia and Egypt. Howbeit news being brought at length that Caesar was arrived at **Tarentum**, and that he came by land unto Brundisium: Cicero departed thence to go meet him, not mistrusting that Caesar would not pardon him, but rather being ashamed to come to his enemy being a conqueror, before such a number of men as he had about him. Yet he was not forced to do or speak anything unseemly to his calling. For Caesar seeing him coming towards him far before the rest that came with him: he lighted from his horse, and embraced him, and walked a great way afoot with him, still talking with him only. And from that time forward he continued to treat him with honour and respect; so that, when Cicero wrote an oration in praise of Cato, Caesar in writing an answer to it, took occasion to commend Cicero's own life and eloquence, comparing him to **Pericles and Theramenes**. Cicero's oration was entitled *Cato*, and Caesar's *Anti-Cato*.

They say further, that **Quintus Ligarius** being accused to have been in the field against Caesar, Cicero took upon him to defend his cause: and that Caesar said unto his friends about him,

> "What hurt is it for us to hear Cicero speak, whom
> we have not heard of long time? For otherwise
> Ligarius (in my opinion) standeth already a
> condemned man, for I know him to be a vile man,
> and mine enemy."

But when Cicero had begun his oration, he moved Caesar marvellously, he had so sweet a grace, and such force in his words: that it is reported Caesar changed divers colours, and showed plainly by his countenance, that there was a marvellous alteration in all the parts of him. For, in the end when the orator came to touch on the Battle of Pharsalia, then was Caesar so troubled, that his body shook withal, and some of the papers he held fell out of his hands; and **he was driven against his will to set Ligarius at liberty**.

Part Four

Afterwards, when the commonwealth of Rome came to be a **kingdom, Cicero leaving to practise any more in the state,** he gave himself to read philosophy to the young men that came to hear him: by whose access unto him (because they were the chiefest of the nobility in Rome) he came again to bear as great sway and authority in Rome, as ever he had done before. His study and endeavour was to write matters of philosophy dialogue-wise, and to translate out of Greek into Latin, taking pains to bring **all the Greek words which are proper unto logic and natural causes**, into Latin. For he it was, as it is said, who first or principally gave Latin names to *phantasia,* *syncatathesis, epokhe, catalepsis, atamon, ameres, kenon,* and other such technical terms, which *[omission]* he succeeded in making intelligible and expressible to the Romans. For his recreation, **he exercised his dexterity** in poetry, and when he was set to it would make five hundred verses in a night.

He spent the greatest part of his time at his country-house near **Tusculum**. He wrote to his friends that he "led **the life of Laertes**," either jestingly, as his custom was, or rather from a feeling of ambition for public employment, which made him impatient under the present state of affairs. He rarely went to the city, unless to pay his court to Caesar.

He was commonly the first amongst those who voted him honours, and sought out new terms of praise for himself and for his actions. As, for example, what he said of the statues of Pompey, which had been thrown down, and were afterwards by Caesar's orders set up again; that Caesar, by this act of humanity, had indeed set up Pompey's statues, but he had fixed and established his own.

Narration and Discussion

"Pompey hath the juster and honester cause of war, but Caesar can better execute," wrote Cicero (North's translation). Might, or right? What would you have done?

Why did Cato say that Cicero had put himself in unnecessary danger by coming to Pompey's camp? How did Cicero react?

Creative narration: Write a letter from Cicero to one of his **Old School Friends**, telling what he has been doing lately.

Lesson Eleven

Introduction

Now in his sixties, Cicero had his share of personal troubles; but the assassination of Julius Caesar brought him out of retirement, and he suddenly found himself competing for power and popularity against Mark Antony.

What did Cicero do after Caesar's assassination?

Julius Caesar had appointed his friends to government positions (magistracies) that should have been elected by the people. After his death, those in those positions were understandably worried that they would lose their jobs. Caesar's assassins were fearful that they would be prosecuted as murderers for what they viewed as an act of patriotism. Cicero persuaded the Senate to leave the magistracies as they were until election time, and to grant an "amnesty" for the assassins. This brought at least a temporary pause to the unrest.

When did Cicero deliver the "Philippics?"

Cicero made the first of the fourteen speeches in September of 44 B.C., which criticized the way that the consuls Dolabella and Mark Antony had miscarried Caesar's will. He urged them to get back to the business of looking after the Roman people.

The "Philippics" continued through April of 43 B.C., and we do not need to go into all of them and their results. Much of the content was against Mark Antony, and in support of "Young Caesar"/Octavius.

The "Ninth Philippic," delivered in February of that year, was a request that the Senate honour Cicero's **Old School Friend** Servius Sulpicius Rufus, who had died while carrying out an embassy to Mark Antony. Here is an excerpt of that speech:

> If all the men of all ages, who have ever had any
> acquaintance with the law in this city, were got
> together into one place, they would not deserve to
> be compared to Servius Sulpicius. Nor was he more
> skillful in explaining the law than in laying down
> the principles of justice. Those maxims which were
> derived from laws, and from the common law, he
> constantly referred to the original principles of
> kindness and equity. Nor was he more fond of
> arranging the conduct of lawsuits than of

preventing disputes altogether. Therefore he is not in want of this memorial which a statue will provide; he has other and better ones. For this statue will be only a witness of his honorable death; those actions will be the memorial of his glorious life. So that this will be rather a monument of the gratitude of the Senate, than of the glory of the man.

Vocabulary

having no necessary thing with him…: he was not well-equipped for the journey

furniture: equipment, supplies

satisfy his creditors: pay off his debts

the "Philippics": Cicero's orations against Antony

of his age: see note in **Lesson Ten**

the conspiracy being executed: Caesar being assassinated

convened the Senate, and made a short address…: see the note "What did Cicero do?" Plutarch says that it was Antony who generally proposed "concord," but that it was Cicero who asked the Senate to grant amnesty to the assassins; and other sources add the clause about not removing those whom Caesar had appointed to various magistracies.

an amnesty: a general pardon

But neither of these things took effect: Plutarch's version of the story calls to mind (and actually inspired) the scenes from Shakespeare's *Julius Caesar*, in which events pile nonstop on top of each other; however, in actual history things moved a bit more slowly, and the attempt at "concord" did last longer than it would seem here.

firebrands: torches

undertaking: intending

some let: some delay

his person: his presence

had contention with Antonius…: Those who have read Genevieve Foster's *Augustus Caesar's World* will remember this dispute over Caesar's estate, and how Octavius asked Cicero for help.

Brutus was highly displeased: This was after the assassination of Julius Caesar, but before the Battle of Philippi.

People

Lentulus (#3) / Dolabella: Publius Cornelius Dolabella, consul in 44 B.C., was the third husband of Cicero's daughter **Tullia**. He is sometimes called **Lentulus** because he was adopted into that family.

Cassius: conspirator against Julius Caesar

Hirtius and Pansa: Aulius Hirtius and Gaius Vibius Pansa Caetronianus, the consuls elected for 43 B.C.

young Caesar: Gaius Octavius or Octavian, called later Caesar Augustus; great-nephew of Julius Caesar; and the first ruler of the Roman Empire

Philippus: Lucius Marcius Philippus, a senator who was the stepfather of Octavius. (His name has nothing to do with Cicero's "Philippics.")

Marcellus: Gaius Claudius Marcellus, a friend of Cicero

Cicero's son: Brutus and his co-conspirator Cassius were in Greece, attempting to get an army together to fight Mark Antony's Roman forces. While they were there, they tutored Cicero's son, who was there at the time studying philosophy and needed help with his Latin and Greek **declamations** (see **Lesson One**).

Historic Occasions

44 B.C.: Julius Caesar and Mark Antony were consuls

March 44 B.C.: the assassination of Julius Caesar

September 44 B.C.: Cicero delivered his first "Philippic"

Early in 43 B.C.: Death of Cicero's friend Sulpicius

Reading

Part One

Cicero had a design, it is said, of writing the history of his country, combining with it much of that of Greece, and incorporating in it all the stories and legends of the past that he had collected. But his purposes were interfered with by various public and various private unhappy occurrences and misfortunes; for most of which he was himself in fault.

For first of all, he did put away his wife Terentia, because she had made but small account of him in all the wars: so that he departed from Rome **having no necessary thing with him to entertain him out of his country**, and yet when he came back again into Italy, she never showed any spark of love or goodwill towards him. For she never came to Brundisium to him, where he remained a long time: and worse than that, his daughter having the heart to take so long a journey in hand to go to him, she (Terentia) neither gave her company to conduct her, nor money or other **furniture** convenient for her; besides, she left him bare walls in his house and nothing in it, and yet greatly brought in debt besides. And these were the causes alleged for their divorce.

But besides that Terentia denied all these, Cicero himself gave her a good occasion to clear herself, because he shortly after married a young maiden, being fallen in fancy with her (as Terentia said) for her beauty: or, as Tyro his servant wrote, for her riches, to the end that with her goods he might pay his debts. For she was very rich, and Cicero also was appointed her guardian, she being left sole heir. Now, because he owed a marvellous sum of money, his parents and friends did counsel him to marry this young maiden, notwithstanding he was too old for her, because that with her goods he might **satisfy his creditors**. But Mark Antony, who mentions this marriage in his answer to **the "Philippics"**, reproaches him for putting away a wife with whom he had lived to older age; adding some happy strokes of sarcasm on Cicero's domestic, inactive, unsoldier-like habits.

Shortly after that he had married his second wife, his daughter Tullia died in child-bed, in **Lentulus' (#3)** house, whose second wife she was, (being before married unto Piso (#2)). So the philosophers and learned men came of all sides to comfort him: but he took her death so sorrowfully, that he put away his second wife, because he thought she did rejoice at the death of his daughter. And thus much touching the state and troubles of his house.

Part Two

He had no concern in the design that was now forming against Caesar, although, in general, he was Brutus' most principal confidant, and one who was as aggrieved at the present, and albeit also he wished for the time past, as much as any other man did. But indeed the conspirators were afraid of his nature, that lacked hardiness; and **of his age**, the which oftentimes maketh the stoutest and most hardiest natures fainthearted and cowardly.

Notwithstanding, **the conspiracy being executed** by Brutus and **Cassius**, Caesar's friends being gathered together, every man was afraid that the city would again fall into civil wars. And Antony also, who was consul at that time, **convened the Senate, and made a short address recommending concord**. And Cicero following with various remarks such as the occasion called for, persuaded the Senate to imitate the Athenians, and decree **an amnesty** for what had been done in Caesar's case, and to bestow provinces on Brutus and Cassius. **But neither of these things took effect.** For the people of themselves were sorry, when they saw Caesar's body brought through the marketplace. And when Antony also did show them his gown all bebloodied, cut, and thrust through with swords: then they were like madmen for anger, and sought up and down the marketplace if they could meet with any of them that had slain him: and taking **firebrands** in their hands, they ran to their houses to set them afire. The conspirators saved themselves: but fearing that if they tarried at Rome, they should have many such alarms, they forsook the city.

Part Three

Antony on this was at once in exultation, and everyone was in alarm with the prospect that he would make himself sole ruler, and Cicero in more alarm than anyone. For Antony, seeing his influence reviving in the commonwealth and knowing how closely he was connected with Brutus, was ill-pleased to have him in the city. Besides, there had been some former jealousy between them, occasioned by the difference of their manners. Cicero, fearing the event, was inclined to go as lieutenant with **Dolabella** into Syria. But **Hirtius and Pansa**, consuls elect as successors of Antony, good men and friends of Cicero, entreated him not to leave them, **undertaking** to put down Antony if he would stay in Rome. And he, neither distrusting wholly, nor trusting them, let Dolabella go without him, promising Hirtius that he would go and spend his summer at Athens, and return again when he entered upon his office.

So he set out on his journey; but some delay occurring in his passage, new intelligence, as often happens, came suddenly from Rome, that Antony had made an astonishing change, and was doing all things and managing all public affairs at the will of the Senate, and that there wanted nothing but his (Cicero's) presence to bring things to a happy settlement. And therefore, blaming himself for his cowardice, he returned again to Rome, and was not deceived in his hopes, at the beginning.. For there came such a number of people out to meet him, that he could do nothing all day long but take them by the hands, and embrace them: who to honour him, came to meet him at the gate of the city, as also by the way to bring him to his house.

Part Four

The next morning Antony assembled the Senate, and called for Cicero by name. Cicero refused to go, and kept his bed, feigning that he was weary with his journey and pains he had taken the day before: but indeed, the cause why he went not, was, for fear and suspicion of an ambush that was laid for him by the way, if he had gone, as he was informed by one of his very good friends. Antony was marvellously offended that they did wrongfully accuse him for laying of any ambush for him: and therefore sent soldiers to his house, and commanded them to bring him by force, or else to set his house afire.

After that time, Cicero and he were always at jar, but yet coldly enough, one of them taking heed of another: until that the **young Caesar** returning from the city of Apollonia, came as lawful heir unto Julius Caesar (the late dictator), and **had contention with Antony for**

the sum of two thousand five hundred myriads, the which Antony kept in his hands of his father's goods. Thereupon, **Philippus**, who had married the mother of this young Caesar, and **Marcellus**, who had also married his sister, went with young Caesar unto Cicero, and there they agreed together, that Cicero should help young Caesar with the favour of his authority and eloquence, as well towards the Senate, as also to the people: and that Caesar in recompense of his goodwill should stand by Cicero with his money and soldiers. For this young Caesar had many of his father's old soldiers about him, that had served under him.

[Omitted for length: Cicero had a special friendship with Octavius ("young Caesar") ever since dreaming about a child who showed great promise, then meeting Octavius and recognizing him as the boy from his dream.]

But in truth, first of all the great malice Cicero bore unto Antony, and secondly his nature that was ambitious of honour, were (in my opinion) the chiefest causes why he became young Caesar's friend: knowing that the force and power of his soldiers would greatly strengthen his authority and countenance in managing the affairs of the state, besides that the young man could flatter him so well, that he called him "father"; at which **Brutus was highly displeased** *[omission]*. Notwithstanding, Brutus took **Cicero's son,** then studying philosophy at Athens, gave him a command, and employed him in various ways, with a good result.

Narration and Discussion

Plutarch skims over the assassination of Julius Caesar. What do you know of these events? How did Cicero fit into the story, and what might that mean for him in the events that followed?

Why did Antony really want Cicero to come back to Rome, rather than going to serve under Dolabella in Syria, or even just to visit Athens for the summer? Would you have gone?

Creative narration: Act out an interview or conversation based on this sentence: "Antony on this was at once in exultation, and everyone was in alarm with the prospect that he would make himself sole ruler, and Cicero in more alarm than anyone."

Lesson Twelve and Examination Questions

Introduction

This lesson includes a long list of **Historic Occasions**, which may seem unusual for a final lesson. They are there for reference, and to help with some of the questions that students may have about this rapidly changing scene. For instance, in April of 43 B.C., Mark Antony was declared an "enemy of the state," so how was it that Cicero was put to death only months later by his doing? The answer is that by October of that year, Mark Antony had formed an alliance with Octavius and Lepidus. (They may not have liked each other much, but each of them had something that the others wanted.) A month later, their Triumvirate was recognized as, more or less, a three-person dictatorship over Rome.

The Triumvirs had one pressing problem: a lack of funds. Following Sulla's earlier example, they declared proscriptions: all "enemies of Caesar" were to be banished or put to death, and their property seized. Cicero was, of course, on the top of Mark Antony's list; and Octavius, however reluctantly, yielded to that demand.

Vocabulary

> **the lictors and ensigns…:** the bodyguards and ceremonial equipment of an army commander

> **Antony had lost the battle, and both the consuls were slain:** see **Historic Occasions**

> **finely served his turn by Cicero's ambition:** underhandedly used Cicero's ambitious nature to serve his own purposes

> **an old man:** see note in **Lesson Ten**

a boy: Octavius was about twenty at this time.

he saw that he had the consulship upon him: see the note under
Historic Occasions

agreed with Antony and Lepidus: formed the **Second Triumvirate**

**Such place took wrath in them as they regarded no kindred nor
blood:** Dryden, "They let their anger and fury take from them the
sense of humanity"

litter: a curtained chair or bed that can be carried

hundred furlongs: 100 furlongs would be 12.5 miles (about 20 km).

he made Cicero's son his colleague and fellow consul with him:
Cicero Minor became a replacement consul partway through 30 B.C.,
and later became governor of Syria and proconsul of Asia.

Etesian winds: the north winds of the Aegean Sea

pulpit for orations: the place where speeches were made

vanquished: conquered, beaten

People

Quintus Pedius: (Not directly named in this text) Nephew of Julius
Caesar. As consul, he passed the *Lex Pedia*, an act calling for the
death of all those involved in or approving of the death of Caesar.
Pedius was expecting a list of only seventeen people, but the Second
Triumvirate used the opportunity to rid themselves of hundreds of
enemies. This took such a toll on Pedius that he died soon
afterwards.

Decimus Junius Brutus Albinus, or **Decimus:** Roman general, cousin
of Marcus Junius Brutus, and governor of Cisalpine Gaul, which
Mark Antony decided should be his province instead.

Historic Occasions

43 B.C.: Mark Antony besieged Mutina (headquarters of **Decimus
Junius Brutus Albinus**)

April, 43 B.C.: Death of the consuls Hirtius and Pansa at the Battle of Mutina; Antony withdrew the siege.

April 21, 43 B.C.: Cicero delivered his final "Philippic," proposing that Mark Antony be declared an enemy of the State. (The Senate agreed.)

May, 43 B.C.: Octavius began secret negotiations with Antony (who had already aligned his forces with those of **Marcus Aemilius Lepidus**) to create a "united Caesarian party"

July, 43 B.C.: Octavius demanded that he be made consul in place of Hirtius and Pansa, and that the "enemy of the State" proclamation against Mark Antony be removed. (The Senate refused.)

August, 43 B.C.: Octavius marched on Rome, and was "elected" consul, along with **Quintus Pedius** (see note under **People**).

October, 43 B.C.: The Second Triumvirate (Octavius, Mark Antony, and Marcus Aemilius Lepidus) met near Bononia

November, 43 B.C.: The Senate formally recognized the Second Triumvirate

43-42 B.C.: The Wars of the Second Triumvirate

December, 43 B.C.: Deaths of Marcus Tullius Cicero and Quintus Tullius Cicero

October, 42 B.C.: The Battle of Philippi and the death of Brutus

31 B.C.: Death of Mark Antony at the Battle of Actium, which confirmed Octavius's uncontested power in Rome

27 B.C.: Octavius wanted to retire from active politics, but the government instead gave him lifelong powers, and the title of **Augustus**, the "elevated" or "divine" one. This also marked the beginning of the **Roman Empire**.

On the Map

Bononia: now Bologna; a city in northern Italy

Astura: or **Torre Astura;** formerly an island, now a peninsula on the coast of **Latium**

Reading

Part One

Now Cicero's great authority and power grew again to be so great in Rome, as ever it was before. For he did what he thought good, and completely overpowered and drove out Antony, and sent the two consuls, Hirtius and Pansa, with an army, to reduce him; and caused the Senate also to decree that young Caesar should have **the lictors and ensigns of a praetor**, as though he were his country's defender.

But after **Antony had lost the battle, and both the consuls were slain**, both the armies came unto Caesar. The Senate then being afraid of this young man that had so great good fortune, they practised by honours and gifts to call the armies from him, which he had about him, and so to diminish the greatness of his power: saying that their country now stood in no need of force, nor fear of defense, since her enemy Antony was fled and gone.

Caesar, fearing this, privately sent some friends to entreat and persuade Cicero to procure that they two together might be chosen consuls, saying he should manage the affairs as he pleased, should have the supreme power, and govern the young man who was only desirous of name and glory. And Caesar himself confessed that, in fear of ruin, and in danger of being deserted, he had **finely served his turn by Cicero's ambition**, having persuaded him to require the consulship, through the help and assistance that he would give him.

And now, more than at any other time, Cicero let himself be carried away and deceived, though he was **an old man**, by the persuasion of **a boy**. He joined him in soliciting votes, and procured the goodwill of the Senate, not without blame at the time on the part of his friends; and he, too, saw soon enough after that he had ruined himself, and betrayed the liberty of his country.

For this young man Octavius Caesar being grown to be very great by his means and procurement: when **he saw that he had the consulship upon him**, he forsook Cicero, and **agreed with Antony and Lepidus**. Then, joining his army with theirs, he divided the empire of Rome with them, as if it had been lands left in common between them: and besides that, there was a bill made of two hundred men and upwards, whom they had appointed to be slain. But the greatest difficulty and difference that fell out between them, was about the outlawing of Cicero. For Antony would hearken to no peace between them, unless Cicero were slain first of all: Lepidus was also in the same mind with Antony: but Caesar was against them both.

Their meeting was by the city of **Bononia**, where they continued three days together, they three only secretly consulting in a place environed about with a little river. Some say that Caesar stuck hard with Cicero the two first days, but at the third, that he yielded and forsook him. The exchange they agreed upon between them, was this. Caesar forsook Cicero: Lepidus, his own brother Paulus: and Antony, Lucius Caesar, his uncle by the mother's side. **Such place took wrath in them, as they regarded no kindred nor blood,** and to speak more properly, they showed that no brute or savage beast is so cruel as man when possessed with power answerable to his rage.

Part Two

While these matters were a-brewing, Cicero was at a house of his in the country, near Tusculum, having at home with him also his brother Quintus Cicero. News being brought them of these proscriptions or outlawries, appointing men to be slain: they determined to go to **Astura,** a place by the seaside where Cicero had another house, there to take sea, and from thence to go into Macedon, unto Brutus, of whose strength in that province news had already been heard. So, they caused themselves to be conveyed thither in two **litters**, both of them being so weak with sorrow and grief, that they could not otherwise have gone their ways. As they were on their way, both their litters going as near to each other as they could, they bewailed their miserable estate: but Quintus chiefly, who took it most grievously. For, remembering that he took no money with him when he came from his house, and that Cicero his brother also had very little for himself: he thought it best that Cicero should hold on his journey, whilst he himself made an errand home to fetch such things as he lacked, and so to make haste again to overtake his brother. They both thought it best so, and then tenderly embracing one another, the tears falling from their eyes, they took leave of each other.

Within a few days after, Quintus Cicero being betrayed by his own servants, unto them that made search for him: he was cruelly slain, and his son with him. But Marcus Tullius Cicero being carried unto Astura, and there finding a ship ready, embarked immediately, and sailed alongst the coast unto Circaeum, having a good gale of wind. There the mariners determining forthwith to make sail again, he came ashore, either for fear of the sea, or for that he had some hope that Caesar had not altogether forsaken him: and therewithal returning towards Rome by land, he had gone about a **hundred furlongs** thence. But then being at a strait how to resolve, and suddenly changing his mind he would needs be carried back again to the sea, where he continued all night marvellous sorrowful, and full of thoughts. Sometimes he resolved to go into Caesar's house privately, and there kill himself upon the altar of his household gods, to bring divine vengeance upon him; but the fear of torture put him off this course.

And after passing through a variety of confused and uncertain counsels, at last he let his servants carry him by sea to Portus Caietae. There he had a very proper pleasant summer house, where the **Etesian winds** do give a trim fresh air in the summer season.

In that place also there is a little temple dedicated unto Apollo, not far from the seaside. From thence there came a great shoal of crows, making a marvellous noise, that came flying towards Cicero's ship, which rowed upon the shoreside. This shoal of crows came and lighted upon the yard of their sail, some crying, and some pecking the cords with their bills: so that every man judged straight, that this was a sign of ill luck at hand. Cicero notwithstanding this, came ashore, and went into his house, and laid him down to see if he could sleep. But the most part of these crows came and lighted upon the chamber window where he lay, making a wonderful great noise: and some of them got unto Cicero's bed where he lay, the clothes being cast over his head, and they never left him, till by little and little they had with their bills plucked off the clothes that covered his face. His servants, seeing this, blamed themselves that they should stay to be spectators of their master's murder, and do nothing in his defense, whilst the brute creatures came to assist and take care of him in his undeserved affliction; so partly by entreaty, and partly by force, they put him again into his litter to carry him to the sea.

Part Three

But in the meantime came the murderers appointed to kill him: Herennius, a centurion, and Popilius Laena, tribune of the soldiers, whom Cicero had formerly defended when prosecuted for the murder of his father. So Cicero's gate being shut, they entered the house by force, and missing him, they asked them of the house what was become of him. They answered, they could not tell. Howbeit there was a young boy in the house called **Philologus**, who had been educated by Cicero in the liberal arts and sciences, and an emancipated slave of his brother Quintus. He told Herennius that Cicero's servants carried him in a litter towards the sea, through dark narrow lanes, shadowed with wood on either side.

The tribune taking a few with him, ran to the place where he was to come out. And Cicero, perceiving Herennius running in the walks, commanded his servants to set down the litter; and taking his beard in his left hand, as his manner was, he stoutly looked the murderers in the faces, his head and beard being all white, and his face lean and wrinkled, for the extreme sorrows he had taken: divers of them that were by, held their hands before their eyes, whilst Herennius did cruelly murder him. So Cicero, being sixty-four years of age, thrust his neck out of the litter, and had his head cut off by Antony's commandment, and his hands also, which wrote "the Philippics" against him [*omission*].

Part Four

When these members of Cicero were brought to Rome, Antony by chance was busily occupied at that time about the election of certain officers: who when he heard of them and saw them, he cried out aloud that now all his outlawries and proscriptions were executed: and thereupon commanded that Cicero's head and his hands should straight be set up over the **pulpit for orations**. This was a sight which the Roman people shuddered to behold, and they believed they saw there, not the face of Cicero, but the image of Antony's own soul.

[*short and gruesome omission about the punishment of Philologus*]

Howbeit I understood that Caesar Augustus, a long time after that, went one day to see one of his nephews, who had a book in his hand of Cicero's; and he, fearing lest his uncle would be angry to find that book in his hands, thought to hide it under his gown. Caesar saw it, and took it from him, and read the most part of it standing, and then delivered it to the young boy, and said unto him: "He was a wise man indeed, my child, and loved his country well." And immediately after he had **vanquished** Antony, being then consul, he made Cicero's son his colleague in the office; and under that consulship the Senate took down all the statues of Antony, and abolished all the other honours that had been given him, and decreed that none of that family should thereafter bear the name of Marcus.

So God's justice made the extreme revenge and punishment of Antony to fall into the house of Cicero. [*Dryden: Thus the final acts of the punishment of Antony were, by the divine powers, devolved upon the family of Cicero.*]

Narration and Discussion

In later years, Augustus Caesar said that Cicero "was a wise man and loved his country well." Do you agree? Why or why not?

For older students: "…they showed that no brute or savage beast is so cruel as man when possessed with power answerable to his rage." Do you agree?

For older students and further thought: Plutarch refers to "God's justice" or "the divine powers." Was there a divine punishment being carried out, and if so, to whom?

Creative narration: There are many possibilities for dramatic presentations in this lesson. If you have only two actors, you might choose the scene between Caesar Augustus and his nephew. News interviews are another possibility.

Examination Questions

For Younger Students

1. Tell the story of how Cicero saved the government (and the city) of Rome from those who wanted to destroy it.

2. "It is reported that the people never passed a thing with so great goodwill, nor so wholly together, as the return of Cicero." Tell the story of his homecoming from banishment.

For Older Students

1. When Cicero was a boy, he hoped "to make the name of the Ciceros noble and famous." Tell one of the ways that he did so.

3. (High School) "For Cicero only of all men in Rome made the Romans know, how much eloquence doth grace and beautify that which is honest, and how invincible right and justice are, being eloquently set forth..." Explain and give examples.

Demetrius

(337 B.C.-283 B.C.)

"But certainly there never was any king upon whom
Fortune made such short turns, nor any other life or
story so filled with her swift and surprising changes,
over and over again, from small things to great,
from splendour back to humiliation and from utter
weakness once more to power and might."

"As, indeed, what other end or period is there of all
the wars and dangers which hapless princes run
into, whose misery and folly it is, not merely that
they make luxury and pleasure, instead of virtue
and excellence, the object of their lives, but that
they do not so much as know where this luxury and
pleasure are to be found?"

(Plutarch's *Life of Demetrius*)

Why study someone with such a negative reputation?

In a prologue which is not included in this text, Plutarch wrote:

We may, I think, avail ourselves of the cases of

those who have fallen into indiscretions, and have, in high stations, made themselves conspicuous for misconduct, and I shall not do ill to introduce a pair or two of such examples among these biographies; not, assuredly, to amuse and divert my readers, or give variety to my theme, but as Ismenias the Theban used to show his scholars good and bad performers on the flute, and to tell them, "You should play like this man," and, "You should not play like that"... So, in the same manner, it seems to me likely enough that we shall be all the more zealous and more emulous to read, observe, and imitate the better lives, if we are not left in ignorance of the blameworthy and the bad.

For this reason, the following book contains the lives of Demetrius Poliorcetes and Antonius the Triumvir; two persons who have abundantly justified the words of Plato, that great natures produce great vices as well as virtues.

Plutarch was also careful to point out the positive aspects of Demetrius' character: for instance, he attempted to preserve the local government and culture of the cities he captured. Plutarch also commended Demetrius for his persistence, energy, wit, and loyalty to his father.

However, as noted elsewhere, this is not a story which should be handed intact to young students.

What was Demetrius' proper name?

Demetrius is more formally known as Demetrius Poliorcetes, or Demetrius I of Macedon. "Poliorcetes" is a **surname**, or additional name, meaning "The Besieger." You may also see it written as Demetrios Poliorketes.

Is it Macedon or Macedonia? Were the Macedonians Greeks?

The names are used interchangeably. Macedonia, or Macedon, was a kingdom in the northeastern part of mainland Greece. The

Macedonians were Greek in many respects, such as religious beliefs; but they valued their distinct heritage and identity.

A Fighting Family

The surname of Demetrius' father Antigonus (#1) was Monopthalmus, meaning "one-eyed." It is believed that he lost an eye when he was struck by a catapult bolt. That, indeed, tells you something about his strength and determination.

Demetrius and his father seem to have had an unusually trusting relationship, as demonstrated by Antigonus' allowing Demetrius to sit near him with a spear (**Lesson One**), and Demetrius' being sent out to fight against Ptolemy at the age of twenty-two (**Lesson Two**). The two fought together on many occasions, although Antigonus did not readily share information or ask opinions from others, including his son. Once, when Demetrius asked when they would be striking camp, Antigonus asked him sarcastically if he was worried about sleeping through the bugle call.

Demetrius' wives...and others

The official wives of Demetrius were (at various times) Phila, Eurydice, Deidamia, Lanassa, and Ptolemais. Not content with those marriages (most of which were made for political reasons), Demetrius had many other involvements which are omitted from this edition.

Demetrius' children

Demetrius had at least three children (some others are named at the end of **Lesson Twelve**). His daughter, Stratonice, from his marriage to Phila, was later married to King Seleucus (**Lesson Six**). His youngest son, called Demetrius the Fair, was born during his marriage to Ptolemais. But it is his older son, Antigonus II Gonatas (#2), whose life may suggest a Creative Narration activity (see **Lesson One**).

A second Demetrius

Demetrius of Phalerum was an Athenian orator and philosopher. He

146

served as the temporary governor of Athens, and he is also mentioned in Plutarch's *Life of Demosthenes*. He will be called Demetrius (#2).

The World of Demetrius

Since his father was both a Macedonian general and a provincial ruler, and then became one of the successors to Alexander's empire, Demetrius grew up in the center of military and political events.

Philip and Alexander

During the years leading up to Demetrius' birth, King Philip II of Macedonia planned to combine his military power with that of the Greek states, mainly to attack the weakening empire of Persia. His assassination in 336 B.C. left that ambition unfulfilled. However, his son Alexander ("The Great") spent the next thirteen years conquering a previously undreamed-of share of the world. When Demetrius was four, his father Antigonus was made governor of Phrygia in the region of Anatolia (now part of Turkey); and Demetrius likely spent some of his childhood there as well.

The Wars of the *Diadochi*

After Alexander's sudden death, his relatives and military colleagues were left to parcel out the pieces of his empire among themselves. This bitter struggle is known as the Wars of the *Diadochi* (pronounced dye-AD-a-kee), meaning "successors," and they can be divided into various groups. There were the remaining members of the Macedonian royal family (see **The Kings of Macedonia**, below). But there were even more determined and powerful competitors in Macedonia, such as Alexander's bodyguards, including Ptolemy and Lysimachus; and the satraps, or governors of provinces, including Antigonus, Seleucus, and Polyperchon. Pyrrhus of Epirus was one of the few non-Macedonians counted in the group. Demetrius and Cassander were considered second-generation members of the *Diadochi*.

(If you have done the *Life of Eumenes* study in the book *The Practical Plutarch*, you can refer to the character cards created there.)

Who was Ptolemy?

Ptolemy I Soter ("Ptolemy the Saviour"), a Macedonian general and friend of Alexander the Great, ruled Egypt after Alexander's death.

Who was Lysimachus?

Lysimachus was king of Thrace. He died in battle in 281 B.C.

Who was Seleucus?

Seleucus I Nicator was a former general in Alexander's army. His territory was the eastern part of the empire, including Babylonia.

Who was Pyrrhus?

Pyrrhus was king of the Molossians, and later of Epirus; his sister Deidamia was married to Demetrius. Lanassa, a later wife of Demetrius, was first married to Pyrrhus.

Who was Cassander?

Cassander was king of Macedonia for several years. Year ago he had been a student of Aristotle, along with Alexander the Great. His father, Antipater (see **Kings of Macedonia**), had also been a close friend of Alexander.

The Kings of Macedonia

King Philip II of Macedonia was succeeded by his son Alexander III (The Great). But what happened after that?

Alexander died without a clear heir to his throne, although his wife was expecting a child. His older half-brother Arrhidaeus became king (he was officially called Philip III), but due to a disability he was unable to carry out his role fully, and most of the decisions were made by regents: Perdiccas, then Antipater, and finally Polyperchon. Antipater's decision to name Polyperchon as the next regent, instead of his son Cassander, caused an ugly power struggle.

Alexander's son, born after his death, also had people who supported his right to the throne over that of his uncle; and after Philip III was put to death in 317 B.C., he became King Alexander IV, and "ruled" until he was murdered in 310 or 309 B.C.

And what about Cassander? He essentially ruled Macedonia from 317 B.C. until he was formally made king in 305; and he died in 297 B.C. It was his son Alexander V (yet another Alexander) who was put to death in 294 B.C. by Demetrius (**Lesson Eight**).

Top Vocabulary Terms in the *Life of Demetrius*

If you recognize these words, you are well on the way to mastering the vocabulary for this study. They will not be repeated in the lessons.

1. **barbarous people, barbarians:** This refers to people who were not Greek, specifically the tribes of the former Persian empire.

2. **citadel:** castle, fortress

3. **confederacy:** joining of military forces; alliance. Those who join together are **confederates**.

4. **countenance:** face

5. **despatch:** an older spelling of dispatch. This has two very different meanings: first, to send something or someone; second, to kill. The only way to tell which is meant is by the context.

6. **engines, engines of battery:** large constructions used to attack enemy fortifications or besiege a city. You may want to look for pictures of Demetrius' *Helepolis*, or "City-Taker."

7. **foot:** foot soldiers, infantry. In the same way, **horse** is often used to refer to soldiers on horseback, or cavalry.

8. **forbear (past tense, forbore):** to restrain or keep oneself from doing something. Note the spelling difference between **forbear** and one's **forebears**, or ancestors.

9. **galley:** a large ship, having sails but generally powered by banks of oars. A **trireme** was a ship with three banks of oars.

10. **garrison:** either a fort, or the soldiers in the fort (often those who

were occupying a town)

11. **javelin:** long spear used for hunting or fighting

12. **spoil, spoils:** treasure, loot; weapons and money taken from an enemy. The word can be either a noun or a verb in the same way as **loot** ("They spoiled/looted the enemy's camp").

13. **talent:** a unit of money, measured by weight. The measure varied according to the time and place, but it was always a very large amount. An Attic (Greek) talent equaled about 57 pounds of gold or silver (25 or 26 kg). Another way to measure its value was in the years it would take a person to earn that much money: one talent would have meant about nine years' earnings for a skilled worker; or a months' pay for a whole **trireme** crew.

Lesson One

Introduction

Demetrius was born into a powerful family in a rapidly changing, unpredictable world; and as he grew up, he accepted the many challenges that came with that position.

Vocabulary

counterfeit to his likeness: do justice to his appearance

vehement: energetic

Bacchus: the Roman name for Dionysus, the Greek god of wine

not so much owing to fear...: his attachment to his father seems to have been from actual love and affection rather than merely because of "fear or duty."

all the successors of Alexander; all the other families: see introductory notes about the *Diadochi*

postulate: (noun) something assumed or believed to be true for the purposes of reasoning.

specimen: example

People

Antigonus (#1): the father of Demetrius (see introductory note)

Philip (#1): the brother of Demetrius. Although we do not know his birthdate, it is recorded that he commanded troops in 310 B.C., four years before his death.

Philip (#2): Philip V of Macedon, the great-grandson of Demetrius, who had his own son put to death for treason

Mithridates: later known as Mithridates I of Pontus

Historic Occasions

c. 382 B.C.: Birth of Antigonus I Monophthalmus

356 B.C.: Birth of Alexander the Great

337 B.C.: Birth of Demetrius I Poliorcetes

336 B.C.: Alexander became king of Macedon

334 B.C.: Alexander began his invasion of the Persian empire

327 B.C.: Alexander began his campaign in India

323 B.C.: Death of Alexander

323-320 B.C.: Antigonus ruled Phrygia, Lycaonia, Pamphylia, Lycia, and western Pisidia, and then became *Strategos* of Asia

c.320 B.C.: Birth of Demetrius' son Antigonus II Gonatas

On the Map

As an introduction to this study, it would be useful first of all to look at a map of Alexander's empire (it was very large!), and then another one showing how it was broken up after his death (when Demetrius was fourteen). A historical atlas will often show a series of such maps, or they can be found online. It is also important to locate **Macedonia** and **Greece**, reviewing cities such as **Athens** and **Corinth** if necessary. The island of **Cyprus** will be mentioned.in **Lesson Two**.

Phrygia: A region of **Anatolia**, part of present-day Turkey.

Pontus: an ancient kingdom in **Cappadocia**

Reading

Part One

Antigonus (#1) had two sons by his wife Stratonice, the daughter of Corraeus: the one of whom, after the name of his uncle, he called Demetrius; the other had that of his grandfather, **Philip (#1)**, and died young. This is the most general account, although some have related that Demetrius was not the son of Antigonus, but of his brother; and that his own father dying young, and his mother being afterwards married to Antigonus, he was accounted to be his son.

Now for Demetrius, though he was a very big man, he was nothing so high as his father, but yet so passing and wonderful fair, that no painter could possibly draw his picture and **counterfeit to his likeness**. For they saw a sweet countenance, mixed with a kind of gravity in his face, a fear with courtesy, and an incomparable princely majesty accompanied with a lively spirit and youth, and his wit and manners were such, that they were both fearful and pleasant unto men that frequented him. For as he was the most easy and agreeable of companions, and the most luxurious and delicate of princes in his drinking and banqueting and daily pleasures, so in action there was never anyone that showed a more **vehement** persistence, or a more passionate energy. **Bacchus**, skilled in the conduct of war, and after war in giving peace its pleasures and joys, seems to have been his pattern among the gods.

He was wonderfully fond of his father Antigonus; and the tenderness he had for his mother led him, for her sake, to redouble attentions, which it was evident were **not so much owing to fear or duty as to the more powerful motives of inclination**. It is reported that, returning one day from hunting, he went unto his father Antigonus, who was conversing with some ambassadors, and after stepping up and kissing his father, he sat down by him, just as he was, still holding in his hand the javelins which he had brought with him. Whereupon Antigonus, who had just dismissed the ambassadors with their answer, called out in a loud voice to them, as they were going, "Mention, also, that this is the way in which we two live together"; as if to imply to them that it was no slender mark of the power and security of his government that there was so perfect good understanding between himself and his son.

Such an unsociable, solitary thing is power, and so much of jealousy and distrust in it, that the first and greatest of the successors of Alexander could make it a thing to glory in that he was not so afraid of his son as to forbid him standing beside him with a weapon in his hand. And, in fact, among **all the successors of Alexander**, that of Antigonus was the only house which, for many descents, was exempted from crime of this kind; or, to state it exactly, **Philip (#2)** was the only one of this family who was guilty of a son's death. **All the other families**, we may fairly say, afforded frequent examples of fathers who brought their children, husbands their wives, children their mothers, to untimely ends; and that brothers should put brothers to death was assumed, like the **postulate** of mathematicians, as the common and recognized royal first principle of safety.

Part Two

Let us here record an example in the early life of Demetrius, showing his natural humane and kindly disposition. It was an adventure which passed between him and **Mithridates**, the son of Ariobarzanes, who was about the same age with Demetrius, and lived with him, in attendance on Antigonus; and although nothing was said or could be said to his reproach, he fell under suspicion, in consequence of a dream which Antigonus had. Antigonus thought himself, in a fair and spacious field, where he sowed golden seed, and saw presently a golden crop come up; of which, however, looking presently again, he saw nothing remain but the stubble, without the ears. And as he stood by in anger and vexation, he heard some voices saying Mithridates had cut the golden harvest and carried it off into **Pontus**.

Antigonus being marvellously troubled with this dream, after he had made his son swear unto him that he would make no man alive privy to that he would tell him: he told him all his dream what he had dreamed, and therewith that he was determined to put this young man Mithridates to death. Demetrius was marvellous sorry for it, and when the young man came, as usual, to pass his time with him, to keep his oath he forbore from saying a word, but, drawing him aside little by little from the company, as soon as they were by themselves, without opening his lips, with the point of his javelin he traced before him the words: "Fly, Mithridates." Mithridates took the hint, and fled by night into **Cappadocia**, where Antigonus's dream about him was quickly brought to its due fulfillment: for he got possession of a large and fertile territory; and from him descended the line of the kings of Pontus, which, in the eighth generation, was reduced by the Romans. This may serve for a **specimen** of the early goodness and love of justice that was part of Demetrius' natural character.

[Omission for length]

Narration and Discussion

Demetrius grew up in a culture full of "jealousy and distrust." How did his family manage to avoid this? How do you think it might affect his life later on?

Does the story of Demetrius and Mithridates have any similarities to that of David and Jonathan (1 Samuel 18-20)?

Creative narration: Demetrius' son Antigonus II Gonatas was born in about 320 B.C. and died at about the age of eighty, in 239 B.C. Although he was raised in a "fighting family," and was a commander of troops, even winning back the Macedonian throne for himself in 277 B.C., his personal interests were more philosophical and literary. Zeno of Citium, the founder of Stoicism, was a favourite guest at court, and Antigonus (#2) wrote letters to Zeno, asking him to help "guide him in virtue" on behalf of his people.

As a single or ongoing activity for this study, create a family history as it might have been told by the younger Antigonus. This could cover many years, or just a short time. It might be a reminiscence in old age, or it could be a letter written in adulthood, or even a school-aged project telling about the people in his family.

As a variation, this activity could be done in dramatized format.

A caveat: Any additional reading on these lives should be overseen by the teacher/parent.

Lesson Two

Introduction

Demetrius, now an eager young commander, was sent out to lead his first battle against his father's rival Ptolemy. He lost spectacularly, but was treated with unusual respect by the enemy, although with an additional message of "now you owe me one." But one defeat was not going to end his career: Demetrius was already aiming at glory.

Vocabulary

the successors of Alexander: see introductory note

occasion of brawl: reasons to fight

near the city of Gaza: see **Historic Occasions**

acceded: agreed

requiting: paying back

Nabataean Arabs: a wealthy tribe living along the Red Sea. Antigonus hoped to add their territory to that which he already controlled in Syria and Phoenicia.

confines: borders

beacon: a light set up as a signal or warning

within a kenning: within range of sight

hurly burly: alarm, confusion

palisade: fence, enclosure

trench: a large ditch surrounding the city, one of the tactics used in siege warfare (see **circumvallation**)

sacked: robbed and ruined

People

Ptolemy, Cassander, Seleucus: see introductory note

Demetrius of Phalerum (#2): see introductory notes

Stilpo the philosopher: a teacher of Zeno (the founder of Stoicism)

Historic Occasions

319-315 B.C.: Seleucus, Ptolemy, Lysimachus, and Cassander formed an alliance to fight against Antigonus

312 B.C.: Demetrius was defeated at the **Battle of Gaza**

311 B.C.: Peace was declared among the *Diadochi*, but it did not last long

309-308 B.C.: Ptolemy took the towns of Lycia and Caria from Antigonus, then seized several Greek cities.

307 B.C.: Demetrius captured **Megara**

On the Map

Review maps of the post-Alexander empire, pointing out **Mesopotamia** (and the river **Euphrates**), **Syria**, and **Babylon**.

Celenae: a town of Phrygia

Mount Caucasus: probably Mount Kazbek, in the Caucasus Mountains

Halicarnassus: a city in Anatolia

Munichia (or **Munychia**): a steep hill in **Piraeus**, the harbour town near Athens

Thebes: a city in **Boeotia**, in central Greece

Megara: an ancient city in west **Attica**, near the island of **Salamis**.

Reading

Part One

Though all **the successors of Alexander** were at continual wars together, yet was it soonest kindled, and most cruel, between them which bordered nearest unto each other, and that by being near neighbours, had always **occasion of brawl** together; as fell out at that time between Antigonus (#1) and **Ptolemy**. News came to Antigonus that Ptolemy had crossed from Cyprus and invaded **Syria**, and was ravaging the country and reducing the cities. Remaining, therefore, himself in Phrygia, he sent Demetrius, now twenty-two years old, to make his first essay as sole commander in an important charge.

But he being a young man, and that had no skill of wars, fighting a battle with an old soldier (trained up in the discipline of wars under Alexander the Great, and that through him, and in his name, had fought many great battles) was soon overthrown, and his army put to flight, **near the city of Gaza**, in which overthrow were slain five thousand men, and almost eight thousand taken. His own tent, also his money, and all his private effects and furniture, were captured. But Ptolemy sent him all his things again, and his friends also that were taken after the battle, with great courteous words: that he would not fight with them for all things together, but only for honour and dominion.

Demetrius accepted the gift, praying only to the gods not to leave him long in Ptolemy's debt, but to let him have an early chance of doing the like to him. He took his disaster, also, with the temper not of a boy defeated in his attempt, but of an old and long-tried general, familiar with reverse of fortune. He used great diligence to gather men again, to make new armours, and to keep the cities and countries in his hands under obedience, and did train and exercise his soldiers in arms, whom he had gathered together.

Antigonus, having news of the overthrow of his son Demetrius, said no more but that Ptolemy had overcome beardless men, and that afterwards he should fight with bearded men. But not to humble the spirit of his son, he **acceded** to his request, and left him to command on the next occasion.

Not long after, Cilles, Ptolemy's lieutenant, with a powerful army, took the field, and looking upon Demetrius as already defeated by the previous battle, he had in his imagination driven him out of Syria before he saw him. But he quickly found himself deceived; for Demetrius came so unexpectedly upon him that he surprised both the general and his army, making him and seven thousand soldiers prisoners of war, and possessing himself of a large amount of treasure. But his joy in the victory was not so much for the prizes he should keep, as for those he could restore; and his thankfulness was less for the wealth and glory than for the means it gave him for **requiting** his enemy's former generosity. He did not, however, take it into his own hands, but wrote to his father. And on receiving leave to do as he liked, he sent back to Ptolemy Cilles and his friends, loaded with presents.

This defeat drove Ptolemy out of Syria, and brought Antigonus from **Celenae** to enjoy the victory and the sight of the son who had gained it.

Part Two

Soon after, Demetrius was sent to bring the **Nabataean Arabs** into obedience. And here he got into a district without water, and incurred considerable danger; but by his resolute and composed demeanour he overawed the barbarians, and returned after receiving from them a large amount of [treasure] and seven hundred camels.

Not long after, Seleucus, whom Antigonus had formerly chased out of **Babylon**, but who had afterwards recovered his dominion by his own efforts and maintained himself in it, went with a great army against the people and nations on the **confines** of India, and the provinces adjoining unto **Mount Caucasus**, to conquer them. Thereupon Demetrius hoping to find **Mesopotamia** without any guard or defense, suddenly passed over the **Euphrates**, and made his way into Babylonia unexpectedly, where he succeeded in capturing one of the two citadels, out of which he expelled the garrison of Seleucus, and placed in it seven thousand men of his own. And after allowing his soldiers to enrich themselves with all the spoil they could carry with them out of the country, he retired to the sea, leaving Seleucus more securely master of his dominions than before, as he seemed by this conduct to abandon every claim to a country which he treated like an enemy's.

Part Three

At his return home, news were brought him that Ptolemy lay at the siege of the city of **Halicarnassus**: whereupon he drew thither with speed to make him raise the siege, and thereby saved the city from him. Now, because by this exploit they won great fame, both of them (Antigonus and Demetrius) fell into a marvellous desire to set all Greece at liberty, which Ptolemy and **Cassander** had everywhere reduced to slavery. Never king took in hand a more honourable nor juster war and enterprise, than that was. For what power or riches he could gather together, in oppressing of the barbarous people, he bestowed it all in restoring the Greeks to their liberty, and only to win fame and honour by it.

So, they being in consultation what way to take, to bring their purpose and desire to pass, and having taken order to begin first at Athens: one of Antigonus' chiefest friends about him told him that he should take the city, and place a good garrison there for themselves, if they could once win it. "For," said he, "it will be a good bridge to pass further into all Greece." Antigonus would not harken to that, but said that the love and goodwill of men was a surer bridge, and that the city of Athens was as a **beacon** to all the land, the which would immediately make his doings shine through the world, as a beacon upon the top of a keep or watchtower.

Thus Demetrius hoisted sail, having five thousand silver talents, and a fleet of two hundred and fifty sail, and sailed towards the city of Athens: in the which **Demetrius of Phalerum (#2)** was governing the city for Cassander, and kept a great strong garrison there within the haven and castle of **Munichia**. By good fortune and skillful management he appeared before **Piraeus**, on the twenty-sixth of Thargelion (now called May), before any man knew of his coming.

Now when this fleet was **within a kenning** of the city, and less, that they might easily see them from thence: every man prepared himself to receive them, taking them to be Ptolemy's ships. But in fine, the captains and governors understanding too late who they were, did what they could to help themselves: but they were all in **hurly burly**, as men compelled to fight out of order, to keep their enemies from landing, and to repulse them, coming so suddenly upon them. Demetrius (#1) having found the entrances of the port open, launched in presently. Then being come to the view of them all, and standing upon the hatches of his galley, he made signs with his hand that he prayed silence.

The tumult being pacified, he caused a herald with a loud voice to make proclamation that his father had sent him in happy hour to deliver the Athenians from all their garrisons, and to restore them again to their ancient liberty and freedom, to enjoy their laws and ancient government of their forefathers. The people, hearing this, at once threw down their shields, and clapping their hands, with loud acclamations entreated Demetrius to land, calling him their deliverer and benefactor. And Demetrius of Phalerum (#2), who saw that there was nothing for it but to receive the conqueror, whether he should perform his promises or not, sent, however, messengers to beg for his protection; to whom Demetrius (#1) gave a kind reception, and sent back with them Aristodemus of Miletus, one of his father's friends. Demetrius of Phalerum, under the change of government, was more afraid of his fellow-citizens than of the enemy; but Demetrius (#1) took precautions for him, and out of respect for his reputation and character, sent him with a safe conduct to **Thebes**, whither he desired to go. For himself, he declared he would not, in spite of all his curiosity, put his foot in the city till he had completed his deliverance by driving out the garrison. So blockading **Munichia** with a **palisade** and **trench**, he sailed off to attack **Megara**, where also there was one of Cassander's garrisons.

[omission for content]

Part Four

The city of Megara was taken and won from Cassander's men, and Demetrius' soldiers would have **sacked** all: howbeit the Athenians made humble intercession for them, that they might not be spoiled. Demetrius (#1) thereupon, after he had driven out Cassander's garrison, he restored it again to her former liberty.

While he was occupied in this, he remembered that **Stilpo the philosopher**, famous for his choice of a life of tranquility, was residing here. He sent for him, and asked him if any of his men had taken anything of his. Stilpo answered him, they had not: "For," quoth he, "I saw no man that took my learning from me."

Pretty nearly all the servants in the city had been stolen away; and so, when Demetrius, renewing his courtesies to Stilpo, on taking leave of him, said unto him, "Well, Stilpo, I leave you your city free." "It is true, O King," quoth he, "for thou hast left us never a slave."

Narration and Discussion

Why did Ptolemy return Demetrius' goods to him, after defeating him? How did Demetrius react to that?

Plutarch describes the goal of setting all the Greek cities at liberty with great admiration: "Never king took in hand a more honourable nor juster war and enterprise, than that was." Why did he say this?

Creative narration #1: Continue the "family history project" as Antigonus II Gonatas might have written it (see **Lesson One**).

Creative narration #2: Dramatize the story of Stilpo the philosopher, or retell it in some other way.

Lesson Three

Introduction

How would you like to be a Tutelary Divinity? How about having your face woven into the Pattern of the Great Robe? Or having a tribe named after you? Or maybe even a month? In this passage, Demetrius and Antigonus were offered all the rewards the grateful Athenians could dream up. But too many honours could also cause problems.

Vocabulary

laid siege to the castle of Munichia: see **Historic Occasions**

razed it to the ground: tore it down

the war of Lamia and the battle before Crannon: The Lamian War, including the Battle of Crannon, was fought from 323-322 B.C.

the government had been administered nominally as an oligarchy: it had (officially) been ruled by a small group of people

odious: offensive

the lineal descendants...: see introductory notes for this study

tutelar, tutelary: protecting, guarding, acting as patron

deity, divinity: a god, one with divine status (Dryden uses both terms)

archon: chief magistrate

were in anxiety...: they were worried about who would win the war

People

Menelaus: King in Cyprus under his brother Ptolemy I Soter.

Historic Occasions

307 B.C.: Demetrius retook Athens (see previous lesson)

307 B.C.: Demetrius married Eurydice

On the Map

Cyprus, Salamis, Corinth: These can be reviewed as needed

Sicyon: a city-state in the northern **Peloponnesus**

Reading

Part One

Shortly after, he returned again unto Athens, and **laid siege to the castle of Munichia**, which he took, and drove out the garrison, and afterwards **razed it to the ground**. After that, through the entreaty and earnest desire of the Athenians, who prayed him to come and refresh himself in their city: he made his entry into it, and caused all the people to assemble, and then restored unto them their ancient laws and the liberty of their country, promising them besides, that he would procure his father to send them a hundred and fifty thousand bushels of wheat, and as much wood and timber as would enable them to build a hundred galleys *[North says a hundred and fifty]*. Thus, the Athenians, through Demetrius' means, recovered the *Democratia* again (to wit, their popular government), fifteen years after they had lost it, from the time of **the war of Lamia and the battle before Crannon**, during which interval of time **the government had been administered nominally as an oligarchy**, but really by a single man, Demetrius of Phalerum (#2) being so powerful.

But by this means they made their saviour and preserver of their country, Demetrius (#1), who seemed to have obtained such honour and glory through his goodness and liberality, hateful and **odious** to all men, for the overgreat and unmeasurable honours which they gave him. For first of all, they called Antigonus (#1) and Demetrius (#1) kings, who before that time had always refused the name, as the one remaining royal honour still reserved for **the lineal descendants of Philip and Alexander**, in which none but they could venture to participate. Another name which they received from no people but the Athenians was that of the **Tutelar Deities** and Deliverers. And to enhance this flattery, by a common vote it was decreed to change the style of the city, and not to have the years named any longer from the annual **archon**; a priest of the two **Tutelary Divinities**, who was to be yearly chosen, was to have this honour, and all public acts and instruments were to bear their date by his name.

They decreed, also, that the figures of Antigonus and Demetrius should be woven, with those of the gods, into the pattern of the Great Robe. They consecrated the spot where Demetrius first alighted from his chariot, and built an altar there, with the name of the Altar of the Descent of Demetrius. They created two new tribes, calling them after the names of these princes, the Antigonid and the Demetriad; and to the council, which consisted of five hundred persons, fifty being chosen out of every tribe, they added one hundred more to represent these new tribes. But yet the strangest act, and most newfound invention of flattery, was that of Stratocles (being the common flatterer and people-pleaser), who put forth this decree, by the which it was ordained that the members of any deputation that the city should send to Demetrius or Antigonus should have the same title, "Ministers of the Sacrifices," as those sent to Delphi or Olympia for the performance of the national sacrifices in behalf of the state at the Greek festivals.

[Omission regarding the character of Stratocles]

And last of all, they changed the name of the month Munychion (to wit, the month of January) and called it Demetrion: and the last day of the month which they called before the new and old moon, they then also called the Demetrion; and they turned the feast of Bacchus, the Dionysia, into the feast of Demetrius.

[Omission for length: further description of these honours]

Thus laying upon Demetrius all these foolish mockeries, who besides was no great wise man, they made him a very fool.

Part Two

Demetrius being at that time at leisure in Athens, **he married a widow called Eurydice**, which came of that noble and ancient house of Miltiades, and had been married before unto one Opheltas, prince of the Cyrenians, and that after his death returned again to Athens. The Athenians were very glad of this marriage, and thought it the greatest honour that came to their city, supposing he had done it for their sakes. But Demetrius was very free in these matters, and was the husband of several wives at once; the highest place and honour among all being retained by Phila, who was Antipater's daughter, and had been the wife of Craterus, the one of all the successors of Alexander who left behind him the strongest feelings of attachment among the Macedonians. And for these reasons Antigonus had obliged him to marry her, notwithstanding the disparity of their years, Demetrius being quite a youth, and she much older.

[Omission for content]

Part Three

While these things passed on in this sort, he was commanded by his father to fight with Ptolemy for the realm of **Cyprus**. So there was no remedy but he must needs obey him, although otherwise he was very sorry to leave the war he had begun (to set the Greeks at liberty), the which had been far more honourable and famous. Before he departed from Athens, he sent unto Cleonides, Ptolemy's general, who was holding garrisons in **Sicyon** and **Corinth**, to offer him money if he would set those cities at liberty. But on his refusal, he set sail hastily, taking additional forces with him, and made for Cyprus; where at his first coming he overcame **Menelaus**, Ptolemy's brother. But shortly after, Ptolemy went thither in person with a great army both by sea and land, and there passed betwixt them fierce threatenings and proud words to each other.

For Ptolemy sent to Demetrius to bid him to depart if he were wise, before all his army came together: which would tread him under their feet, and march upon his belly, if he tarried their coming. Demetrius on the other side sent him word, that he would do him this favour to let him escape, if he would swear and promise unto him to withdraw his garrisons which he had in the cities of Corinth and Sicyon. And not they alone, but all the other potentates and princes of the time **were in anxiety for the uncertain impending issue of the conflict**; as it seemed evident that the conqueror should not only be lord of the realm of Cyprus and Syria, but therewith also of greater power than all the rest.

Narration and Discussion

How did the honour shown to Demetrius make him "hateful and odious?"

Creative narration #1: This lesson lends itself well to dramatization or other creative activities about the honouring of Antigonus and Demetrius. One suggestion might be to create some "merchandise" or souvenirs (realistic, or anachronistic such as t-shirts).

Creative narration #2: Continue the "family history project" as Antigonus II Gonatas might have written it.

For further thought: Throughout this *Life*, we are reminded of the good qualities in Demetrius, such as his vision of restoring liberty in the cities he conquered, and his obedience when he was commanded to fight Ptolemy again. However, Plutarch admits here that Demetrius was "no great wise man," and that "all these foolish mockeries...made him a very fool." Dryden translates it this way: "With this befooling they completed the perversion of a mind which even before was not so strong or sound as it should have been." What does the Bible say about listening to flatterers? (Prov. 26:28, 29:5)

Lesson Four

Introduction

Demetrius took his ships to Salamis, against those of Ptolemy. His father Antigonus was left at home, biting his nails and hoping for good news. But when the news did finally come, one little word attached to it changed their lives forever.

Vocabulary

sally: charge; move out suddenly and forcefully

impetuosity: this usually means without giving something proper consideration, but in this case it means more like "without giving it another thought"

routed: defeated

military engines: see introductory vocabulary notes

thou hast kept us in a trance a good while: Dryden says, "as you chose to torture us so long for your good news"

royal band or diadem: coronet, crown

made them stand upon themselves: made them proud and arrogant

dissemble: the modern meaning of this word is to do something falsely, but in this context it means to ignore, let pass unnoticed

familiars: friends

Historic Occasions

306 B.C.: Demetrius defeated Ptolemy and Menelaus at Salamis, and also conquered Cyprus. Following this victory, Antigonus declared both himself and Demetrius to be kings, and the other *Diadochi* (such as Lysimachus) followed suit.

306 B.C.: Death of Demetrius' brother Philip

On the Map

Miletus: a city of Anatolia

Reading

Part One

Ptolemy had brought a hundred and fifty galleys with him, and gave orders to Menelaus to **sally**, in the heat of the battle, out of the harbour of Salamis, and attack with sixty ships the rearward of Demetrius' ships, to break their order. Demetrius, on the other side, opposing these sixty with ten of his galleys, which were a sufficient number to block up the narrow entrance of the harbour, and drawing out his land forces along all the headlands running out into the sea, went into action with a hundred and eighty galleys, and, attacking with the utmost boldness and **impetuosity**, utterly **routed** Ptolemy, who fled with eight ships, the sole remnant of his fleet, seventy having been taken with all their men, and the rest destroyed in the battle; while the whole multitude of attendants, friends, and women, that had followed in the ships of burden, all the arms, treasure, and **military engines**, fell, without exception, into the hands of Demetrius, and were by him collected and brought into the camp.

[Omission for content]

After this victory by sea, Menelaus made no more resistance, but yielded up Salamis and his ships unto Demetrius, and put into his hands also twelve hundred horsemen, and twelve thousand footmen, well-armed. But that which added more than all to the glory and splendour of the success was the humane and generous conduct of Demetrius to the vanquished. For, after he had given honourable funerals to the dead, he bestowed liberty upon the living; and that he might not forget the Athenians, he sent them, as a present, complete arms for twelve hundred men.

To carry this happy news, Aristodemus of **Miletus**, the most perfect flatterer belonging to the court, was despatched to Antigonus; and he, to enhance the welcome message, was resolved, it would appear, to make his most successful effort. For when he had taken land after he was come out of the isle of Cyprus, he would in no wise have the ship he came in to come near the shore, but commanded them to ride at anchor, and no man to leave the ship; but he himself got into a little boat, and went unto Antigonus, who all this while was in marvellous fear and perplexity for the success of this battle, as men may easily judge they are which hope after so great uncertainties. Now when word was brought him that Aristodemus was coming to him all alone, it put him into yet greater trouble; he could scarcely forbear from going out to meet him himself; he sent messenger on messenger, and friend after friend, to inquire what news, and to bring him word presently again how the world went.

But not one of them could get anything out of him, for he went on still fair and softly with a sad countenance, and very demurely, speaking never a word. Wherefore Antigonus' heart being cold in his belly, he could stay no longer, but would himself go and meet with Aristodemus at the gate, who had a marvellous press of people following on him, besides those of the court which ran out to hear his answer. At length when he came near unto Antigonus, holding out his right hand unto him, he cried out aloud, "God save thee, O King Antigonus: we have overcome King Ptolemy in battle by sea, and have won the realm of Cyprus, with sixteen thousand eight hundred prisoners."

Then answered Antigonus, "And God save thee too: truly, Aristodemus, **thou hast kept us in a trance a good while**, but to punish thee for the pain thou hast put us to, thou shalt the later receive the reward of thy good news."

Part Two

Then was the first time that the people with a loud voice called Antigonus and Demetrius "kings." Now for Antigonus, his friends and familiars did at that present instant put on the **royal band or diadem** upon his head: But for Demetrius, his father sent it unto him, and by his letters called him "king." And, because it should not seem that for one overthrow received, their hearts were dead, Ptolemy's followers also took occasion to bestow the style of king upon him [Ptolemy]; and the rest of the successors of Alexander were quick to follow the example. Lysimachus began to wear the diadem, and Seleucus, who had before received the name in all addresses from the barbarians, now also took it upon him in all business with the Greeks. Cassander still retained his usual superscription in his letters, but others, both in writing and speaking, gave him the royal title.

Now this was not only an increase of a new name, or changing of apparel, but it was such an honour, as it lifted up their hearts, and **made them stand upon themselves**: and besides it so framed their manner of life and conversation with men, that they grew more proud and stately, than ever they were before: like unto common players of tragedies, who appareling themselves to play their parts upon the stage, do change their gait, their countenance, their voice, their manner of sitting at the table, and their talk also. So that afterwards they grew more cruel in commanding their subjects, when they had once taken away that modest style under which they formerly **dissembled** their power, which before made them far more lowly and gentle in many matters unto them. And all this came through one vile flatterer, that brought such a wonderful change in by the world.

Antigonus therefore, puffed up with the glory of the victory of his son Demetrius, for the conquest of Cyprus: he determined forthwith to set upon Ptolemy. He himself led the army by land, having his son Demetrius still rowing by the shoreside with a great fleet of ships. But one of his **familiars**, called Medius, being asleep had a vision one night that told him what should be the end and success of this journey. He thought he saw Antigonus and his whole army running, as if it had been a race, and that at the first he ran with great force and swiftness: but that afterwards his strength and breath failed him so much, that when he should return, he had scant any pulse or breath, and with much ado retired again. And even so it chanced unto him. For Antigonus met with many difficulties by land; and Demetrius, encountering a great storm at sea, was driven, with the loss of many of his ships, upon a dangerous coast without a harbour. So the expedition returned without effecting anything.

Narration and Discussion

Describe the epidemic of "kingliness" that broke out among the rulers at that time. Why does Plutarch blame it all on "one vile flatterer?"

Creative narration #1: Act out the scene between Antigonus and Aristodemus. Which of them had the last laugh?

Creative narration #2: Continue the "family history project."

Lesson Five

Introduction

Antigonus, aging and less able to fight, was willing to overlook his son's personal failings because of his many talents. Demetrius was turning out to be a born engineer, as well as a good military leader. After he used his siege engines to subdue the Rhodians, they asked if he would please leave them some of the machinery, as a memorial both to their courage and his power.

Vocabulary

corpulence: weight

sober and continent: self-restrained, moderate in habits

not to be satiated: he could never have enough of this

machines: see introductory vocabulary notes

turning: woodworking

cuirass: a piece of body armour

style or graver: a tool with a hard point used for writing or engraving

the honourable example of the Athenians: this is a flashback to the days of King Philip

affront: insult, offense

Minerva: the Roman name for Athena, the patron goddess of Athens

People

Lysimachus: one of the *Diadochi* (see introductory notes)

Protogenes the Caunian: a famous Greek artist

Ialysus: a legendary Rhodian hero

Apelles: a rival painter

Historic Occasions

305-304 B.C.: The Siege of Rhodes

302 B.C.: Demetrius returned to Greece

On the Map

Cilicia: a region of southern Anatolia

Rhodes (Rhodians): a large island in the Aegean Sea, and the city by that name

Heraclea: a city-state near **Thermopylae**

Reading

Part One

Antigonus (#1), now nearly eighty years old, was no longer well able to go through the fatigues of a marching campaign, though rather on account of his great size and **corpulence** than from loss of strength; and for this reason he left things to his son, whose fortune and experience appeared sufficient for all undertakings, and whose luxury and expense and revelry gave him no concern. For in time of peace, he [Demetrius] was given over to all those vices; but in time of war, he was as **sober and continent** as any man so born by nature.

[Omission for content]

So Antigonus did gently bear with his son's faults, in respect of the many other virtues he had. The Scythians in their drinking bouts, twang their bows to keep their courage awake amidst the dreams of indulgence; but he [Demetrius] would resign his whole being, now to pleasure, and now to action; and though he never let thoughts of the one intrude upon the pursuit of the other, yet when the time came for preparing for war, he showed as much capacity as any man.

And indeed his ability displayed itself even more in preparing for than in conducting a war. He thought he could never be too well supplied for every possible occasion, and took a pleasure, **not to be satiated**, in great improvements in ship-building and **machines**. He did not waste his natural genius and power of mechanical research on toys and idle fancies, **turning**, painting, and playing on the flute, like some kings.

[omitted for length: descriptions of the hobbies of various kings]

But when Demetrius played the workman, it was like a king, and there was magnificence in his handicraft. The articles he produced bore marks upon the face of them not of ingenuity only, but of a great mind and a lofty purpose. They were such as a king might not only design and pay for, but use his own hands to make; and while friends might be terrified with their greatness, enemies could be charmed with their beauty; a phrase which is not so pretty to the ear as it is true to the fact. The very people against whom they were to be employed could not forbear running to gaze with admiration upon his galleys of five and six ranges of oars, as they passed along their coasts; and the inhabitants of besieged cities came on their walls to see the spectacles of his famous **City-Takers**.

For **Lysimachus**, who of all other kings did malice Demetrius most, coming to raise the siege from the city of Soli in **Cilicia**, sent first to desire permission to see his galleys and engines, and, having had his curiosity gratified by a view of them, expressed his admiration and quitted the place. The **Rhodians**, also, whom he long besieged, begged him, when they concluded a peace, to let them have some of his engines, which they might preserve as a memorial at once of his power and of their own brave resistance.

Part Two

The quarrel between Demetrius and the Rhodians was on account of their being allies to Ptolemy, and in the siege the greatest of all the engines was planted against their walls. The base of it was square, each side containing twenty-four cubits; it rose to a height of thirty-three cubits, growing narrower from the base to the top. Within were several apartments or chambers, which were to be filled with armed men, and in every story the front towards the enemy had windows for discharging missiles of all sorts, the whole being filled with soldiers for every description of fighting. And what was most wonderful was that, notwithstanding its size, when it was moved it never tottered or inclined to one side, but went forward on its base in perfect equilibrium, with a loud noise and great impetus, astounding the minds, and yet at the same time charming the eyes of all the beholders.

Whilst Demetrius was at this same siege, there were brought to him two iron **cuirasses** from Cyprus, weighing each of them no more than forty pounds; and Zoilus, who had forged them, to show the excellence of their temper, desired that one of them might be tried with a catapult missile, shot out of one of the engines at no greater distance than six-and-twenty paces; and, upon the experiment, it was found that though the dart exactly hit the cuirass, yet it made no greater impression than such a slight scratch as might be made with the point of a **style or graver**. Demetrius took this for his own wearing, and gave the other to Alcimus the Epirot, the best soldier and strongest man of all his captains, the only one who used to wear armour to the weight of two talents, one talent being the weight which others thought sufficient. (He fell during this siege, in a battle near the theatre.)

The Rhodians made a brave defense, insomuch that Demetrius saw he was making but little progress, and only persisted out of obstinacy and passion; and the rather because the Rhodians, having captured a ship in which some clothes and furniture, with letters from herself, were coming to him from Phila his wife, had sent on everything to Ptolemy, and had not copied **the honourable example of the Athenians**, who, having surprised an express sent from King Philip, their enemy, opened all the letters he was charged with, excepting only those directed to Queen Olympias, which they returned with the seal unbroken.

Yet, although greatly provoked, Demetrius, into whose power it shortly after came to repay the **affront**, would not suffer himself to retaliate. **Protogenes the Caunian** had been making them a painting of the story of **Ialysus**, which was all but completed, when it was taken by Demetrius in one of the suburbs. The Rhodians thereupon sending a herald unto him, to beseech him to spare the defacing of so goodly a work: he returned them answer, that he would rather suffer his father's images to be burnt, than a piece of art which had cost so much labour. It is said to having Protogenes seven years to paint, and they tell us that **Apelles**, when he first saw it, was struck dumb with wonder, and called it, on recovering his speech, "a great labour and a wonderful success," adding, however, that it had not the graces which carried his own paintings as it were up to the heavens. This picture, which came with the rest in the general mass to Rome, there perished by fire.

Part Three

Now as the Rhodians were desirous to be rid of this war, and that

Demetrius also was willing to take any honest occasion to do it: the ambassadors of the Athenians came happily to serve both their desires, who made peace between them with these conditions: that the Rhodians should bind themselves to aid Antigonus (#1) and Demetrius against all enemies, Ptolemy excepted.

The Athenians entreated his help against Cassander, who was besieging the city. So he went thither with a fleet of three hundred and thirty ships, and many soldiers; and not only drove Cassander out of Attica, but pursued him as far as **Thermopylae**, routed him and became master of **Heraclea**, which came over to him voluntarily, and of a body of six thousand Macedonians, which also joined him. Returning hence, he gave their liberty to all the Greeks on this side of Thermopylae, and made alliance with the Boeotians, took Cenchrae; and reducing the fortresses of Phyle and Panactum, in which were garrisons of Cassander, restored them to the Athenians.

Therefore though it seemed the Athenians had before bestowed to their uttermost power all kinds of honours that could be offered him, every man striving for life to prefer the same: yet they found out new devices to flatter and please him. For they ordained that the place behind the temple of **Minerva**, called the Parthenon *[omission]* should be prepared as a house for him to lie in: and so they said that the goddess Minerva did lodge him with her *[omission for content]*.

Narration and Discussion

"For his friends did not only wonder at their greatness, but his very enemies also were delighted with the beauty of them." Are there any military weapons (past or present) that might charm you with their beauty?

"Yet, although greatly provoked, Demetrius, into whose power it shortly after came to repay the affront, would not suffer himself to retaliate." Why not?

For further thought: Plutarch says that Demetrius "did not waste his natural genius and power of mechanical research on toys and idle fancies, turning, painting, and playing on the flute, like some kings." Is he saying that painting and playing on the flute are "idle fancies" for everyone, or only for kings? Do you agree? (Consider what Demetrius had to say about the painting by Protogenes.)

For older students and further thought: In Part One, how well did Demetrius seem to be able to control his use of alcohol and other distractions? If you have read Charlotte Mason's writings on the Will, how does Plutarch's description of Demetrius meet the requirements of Will, such as having an object outside of oneself?

Creative narration: Continue the "family history project."

Lesson Six

Introduction

Cassander, Seleucus, Ptolemy, and Lysimachus had already achieved political and military power; but now, along with Antigonus and Demetrius, they viewed themselves as kings; and Antigonus found himself at war with the other "kings." After a variety of disputes over territories and borders, things came to the point where Antigonus had to bring Demetrius back from Greece (where he had been battling against Cassander), to help him fight Lysimachus. In the previous lesson, we were told that "Antigonus, now nearly eighty years old, was no longer well able to go through the fatigues of a marching campaign…." However, he decided to push himself to fight in person at the Battle of Ipsus.

Vocabulary

> **Feast of Juno:** The Heraea, a festival held at Argos every five years in honour of the goddess Hera (called Juno by the Romans), which included athletic games
>
> **concourse:** meeting, assembly
>
> **comic, comedy:** a play with a happy ending (vs. a tragedy)
>
> **trifling concessions:** small compromises

contempt: scorn

composure: calmness

Jupiter: the god Zeus

lost him the day: lost him the battle

the main battle of Antigonus: his troops

fidelity: faithfulness, loyalty

People

Antiochus the son of Seleucus: Antiochus I Soter

Historic Occasions

301 B.C.: The armies of Cassander, Seleucus, and Lysimachus fought Demetrius and Antigonus at the Battle of Ipsus

301 B.C.: Death of Antigonus, and the breakup of his territories. Demetrius' mother Stratonice fled to the island of Salamis.

300 B.C.: Demetrius took his daughter, also named Stratonice, to Rhodes, to be married to Seleucus

On the Map

Peloponnesus or **Peloponnese:** the southern half of Greece, below the **Isthmus of Corinth** (the strip of land joining the two parts together)

Acte: the peninsula containing **Mount Athos**, in northeastern Greece

Arcadia: a region in the central **Peloponnese**

Mantinea: a city of **Arcadia**

Argos: a city in the **Peloponnese**, known for being one of the oldest continuously inhabited cities in the world

Sicyon: a city-state in the northern **Peloponnese**. It was renamed

Demetrias for a short time, but then returned to its old name.

Molossians: a tribe of the region of **Epirus** in northwestern Greece

Ephesus: A Greek city on the coast of **Ionia**; located in present-day Turkey

Chersonesus or **Chersonese:** A Greek colony which was located in the southwestern part of the Crimean Peninsula

Reading

Part One

Between Lessons Five and Six is a passage about Demetrius' defilement of the temple. Please leap over it if you are reading from or listening to a complete text.

After this Demetrius marched with his forces into **Peloponnesus**, where he met with none to oppose him, his enemies fleeing before him, and allowing the cities to join him. He received into friendship all **Acte**, as it is called, and all **Arcadia** except **Mantinea**. He bought the liberty of **Argos**, Corinth, and **Sicyon**, by paying a hundred talents to their garrisons to evacuate them.

At Argos, during the **Feast of Juno**, which happened at the time, he presided at the games, and, joining in the festivities with the multitude of the Greeks assembled there, he celebrated his marriage with Deidamia, daughter of Aeacides, king of the **Molossians**, and sister of Pyrrhus.

At Sicyon he told the people they had put the city just outside of the city, and, persuading them to remove to where they now live, gave their town not only a new site but a new name, Demetrias, after himself.

A general assembly met on **the Isthmus**, where he was proclaimed, by a great **concourse** of the people, the "Commander of Greece," like Philip and Alexander of old; whose superior he, in the present height of his prosperity and power, was willing enough to consider himself. And certainly, in one respect, he outdid Alexander, who never refused that title to other kings, or took on himself the style of "king of kings," though many kings received both their title and their authority as such from him; whereas Demetrius used to ridicule those who gave the name of king to any except himself and his father; and in his entertainments was well pleased when his followers, after drinking to him and his father as kings, went on to drink the health of Seleucus, with the title of "Master of the Elephants"; of Ptolemy, by the name of "High Admiral"; of Lysimachus, with the addition of "Treasurer"; and of Agathocles, with the style of "Governor of the Island of Sicily."

The other kings merely laughed when they were told of his vanity; Lysimachus alone expressed some indignation.

[Omission for length and content]

Part Two

And now the story passes from the **comic** to the tragic stage in pursuit of the acts and fortunes of its subjects.

A general league of the kings, who were now gathering and combining their forces to attack Antigonus (#1), recalled Demetrius from Greece. He was encouraged by finding his father full of a spirit and resolution for the combat that belied his years. Yet it would seem to be true, that if Antigonus could only have borne to make some **trifling concessions**, and if he had shown any moderation in his passion for empire, he might have maintained for himself till his death and left to his son behind him the first place among the kings. But he was of a violent and haughty spirit; and the insulting words as well as actions which he allowed himself could not be borne by young and powerful princes, and provoked them into combining against him. Though now when he was told of the confederacy, he could not forbear from saying that this flock of birds would soon be scattered by one stone and a single shout.

Antigonus took the field at the head of more than seventy thousand foot, and of ten thousand horse, and seventy-five elephants. His enemies had sixty-four thousand foot and five hundred more horse than he; elephants to the number of four hundred, and a hundred and twenty chariots. When the two armies were one near unto the other, methinks he had some imagination in his head that changed his hope, but not his courage. For whereas in all former campaigns he had ever shown himself lofty and confident, loud in voice and scornful in speech, often by some joke or mockery on the eve of battle expressing his **contempt** and displaying his **composure**, he was now remarked to be thoughtful, silent, and retired.

One day he called all his army together, and presented his son unto the soldiers, recommending him unto them as his heir and successor, and talked with him alone in his tent. Whereat men marvelled the more, because that he never used before to impart to any man the secrets of his counsel and determination, no not to his own son, but did all things of himself: and then commanded that thing openly to be done, which he had secretly purposed. For proof hereof it is said, Demetrius being but a young man, asked him on a time when the camp should remove: and that Antigonus in anger answered him, "Art thou afraid thou shalt not hear the sound of the trumpet?"

Furthermore, there fell out many ill signs and tokens that killed their hearts. Demetrius, in a dream, had seen Alexander, completely armed, appear and demand of him what word they intended to give in the time of the battle; and Demetrius answering that he intended the word should be "**Jupiter** and Victory." "Then," said Alexander, "I will go to your adversaries and find my welcome with them." And afterwards, at the very day of the overthrow, when all their army were set in battle array, Antigonus coming out of his tent, had such a great fall, that he fell flat on his face on the ground, and hurt himself very sorely. And on recovering his feet, lifting up his hands to heaven, he prayed the gods to grant him, "either victory, or death without knowledge of defeat."

Part Three

When the armies engaged, Demetrius, who commanded the greatest and best part of the cavalry, made a charge on **Antiochus the son of Seleucus**; and, gloriously routing the enemy, followed the pursuit, in the pride and exultation of success, so eagerly, and so unwisely far, that it fatally **lost him the day**; for when, perceiving his error, he would have come in to the assistance of his own infantry, he was not able, the enemy with their elephants having cut off his retreat.

On the other hand, Seleucus, observing **the main battle of Antigonus** left naked of their horse, did not charge, but made a show of charging; and keeping them in alarm and wheeling about and still threatening an attack, he gave opportunity for those who wished it to separate and come over to him; which a large body of them did, the rest taking to flight.

But the old King Antigonus still kept his post, and when a strong body of the enemies drew up to charge him, and one of those about him cried out to him, "Sir, they are coming upon you," he only replied, "What else should they do? But Demetrius will come to my rescue." *[North: He answered again: "But how should they know me? And if they did, my son Demetrius will come and help me."]* And in this hope he persisted to the last, looking out on every side for his son's approach, until he was borne down by a whole multitude of darts, and fell. His other followers and friends fled, and Thorax of Larissa remained alone by the body.

Now the battle having such success as you have heard, the kings and princes that had won so glorious a victory, as if they had cut a great body in sundry pieces; so they divided Antigonus' kingdom among them, and every man had his part of all the provinces and countries which Antigonus kept, adding that unto their other dominions which they possessed before. As for Demetrius, with five thousand foot and four thousand horse, he fled at his utmost speed to **Ephesus**, where it was the common opinion he would seize the treasures of the temple to relieve his wants; but he, on the contrary, fearing such an attempt on the part of his soldiers, hastened away, and sailed for Greece, his chief remaining hopes being placed in the **fidelity** of the Athenians, with whom he had left part of his navy, and of his treasures, and his wife Deidamia. And in their attachment he had not the least doubt but he should in this his extremity find a safe resource.

[Omitted for length: After losing this battle and his kingdom, Demetrius expected to find safety in Athens, but was told that the Athenians had just passed a law "to suffer no more kings to come into Athens." He reclaimed his large galley, but otherwise had trouble in trying to round up even his own troops.]

He therefore took his course to the **Chersonesus**, where he ravaged the territories of Lysimachus, and by the spoils which he took, maintained and kept together his troops, which were now once more beginning to recover and to show some considerable front. Nor did any of the other princes care to meddle with him on that side; for

Lysimachus had quite as little claim to be loved, and was more to be feared for his power.

[Omission for length]

Narration and Discussion

How did Demetrius' dream about Alexander affect his actions?

Plutarch says that the story here turns from comic to tragic. What does he mean? (A "comedy" was not necessarily humorous, but a story in which the characters triumphed over adversity.)

Creative narration #1: Although Demetrius had lost his father and his kingdom, the passage ends on a more positive note. If he had been interviewed at this time, what might he have said about his current situation and his plans for the future?

Creative narration #2: Continue the "family history project." What might Antigonus (#2) write as a tribute to his grandfather?

Lesson Seven

Introduction

Relations between Demetrius, Seleucus, and the other *Diadochi* continued to go up and down. Demetrius allowed Seleucus to marry his daughter Stratonice, and at first that new alliance seemed to go well. However, mistrust and jealousy lurked beneath the surface courtesies.

One major event at this time was the Siege of Athens, in 287 B.C. Athens, under a tyrant ruler named Lachares, had attacked the Macedonian garrison; and Demetrius successfully besieged the city. But he had plans for more, including the unheard-of capture of Sparta; and even to retake his own kingdom of Macedonia. As Plutarch says of him,

> But certainly there never was any king upon whom

Fortune made such short turns, nor any other life or
story so filled with her swift and surprising changes,
over and over again, from small things to great,
from splendour back to humiliation and from utter
weakness once more to power and might...

Vocabulary

he should marry his daughter Ptolemais: this did not happen until
sometime later

usurper: someone who takes a position illegally or by force

in a petty manner: with brief battles and raids

divers: various

straiten: put someone into a tight place

corn: grain

a proportion: a small number

consternation: state of dismay and upset

in the pulpit for orations: on the speakers' platform

preferring: proposing

which might give him the trouble of quitting his other enterprises:
Demetrius was hoping Athens would remain peaceful so that he
could focus on his other problems.

his mother and children: It is not clear which children are referred to.

recompense for his succour: reward for his trouble

People

Lachares: a political leader in Athens, who had expelled **Demochares**,
the leader of an opposing party, and had taken sole power

Epicurus: famous philosopher, founder of Epicureanism

Archidamus: Archidamus IV, one of the kings of Sparta at the time (Sparta had an unusual tradition of having two kings at once.)

Historic Occasions

297 B.C.: Death of Cassander

294 B.C.: Demetrius took power in Athens

On the Map

Tyre and **Sidon:** coastal cities which are now part of Lebanon

Attica: the region of Athens

Messene: a city in the Peloponnese (not to be confused with Messina in Sicily)

Laconia: the region around the city of **Sparta** (Sparta was also called **Lacedaemon**)

Dium: a port city of Macedonia

Reading

Prologue

[Omission for length: see notes above]

Not long after this, Demetrius' wife Deidamia contracted an illness, of which she died. After her death, Demetrius, by the mediation of Seleucus, became reconciled to Ptolemy, and an agreement was made that **he (Demetrius) should marry his daughter Ptolemais**.

Thus far all was handsomely done on the part of Seleucus. But, shortly after, desiring to have the province of Cilicia from Demetrius for a sum of money, and being refused it, he then angrily demanded of him the cities of **Tyre** and **Sidon**, which seemed a mere piece of arbitrary dealing, and, indeed, an outrageous thing, that he, who was possessed of all the vast provinces between India and the Syrian sea, should think himself so poorly off as, for the sake of two cities which he coveted, to disturb the peace of his "dear connection," already a sufferer under a severe reverse of fortune. However, he did but justify the saying of Plato, that the only certain way to be truly rich is not to have more property, but fewer desires. For whoever is always grasping at more avows that he is still in want, and must be poor in the midst of affluence.

But Demetrius, whose courage did not sink, resolutely sent him answer that, though he were to lose ten thousand battles like that of Ipsus, he would pay no price for the goodwill of such a son-in-law as Seleucus. He reinforced those cities with sufficient garrisons to enable them to make a defense against Seleucus, and, receiving information that **Lachares**, taking the opportunity of their civil dissensions, had set himself up as a **usurper** over the Athenians, he imagined that if he made a sudden attempt upon that city, he might now without difficulty get possession of it.

Part One

Demetrius crossed the sea in safety with a large fleet; but passing along the coast of **Attica**, was met by a violent storm, and lost the greater number of his ships, and a very considerable body of men on board them. As for him, he escaped, and began to make war **in a petty manner** with the Athenians, but, finding himself unable to effect his design, he sent back orders for raising another fleet, and, with the troops which he had, marched into Peloponnesus and laid siege to the city of **Messene**. In attacking that place, he was in danger of death; for a missile from an engine struck him in the face, and passed through the cheek into his mouth.

He recovered, however, and as soon as he was in a condition to take the field, won over **divers** cities which had revolted from him, and made an incursion into Attica, where he took Eleusis and Rhamnus, and wasted the country thereabout. And that he might **straiten** the Athenians by cutting off all manner of provision, a vessel laden with **corn** bound thither falling into his hands, he ordered the [officers] to be immediately hanged, thereby to strike terror into others, that so they might not venture to supply the city with provisions. By which means they were reduced to such extremities that a bushel of salt sold for forty drachmas, and a peck of wheat for three hundred. Ptolemy had sent to their relief a hundred and fifty galleys, which came so near as to be seen off Aegina; but this brief hope was soon extinguished by the arrival of three hundred ships, which came to reinforce Demetrius, from Cyprus, Peloponnesus, and other places; upon which Ptolemy's fleet took to flight, and Lachares, the tyrant, ran away, leaving the city to its fate.

Now the Athenians, who before had commanded, upon pain of death, that no man should make any motion to the council to treat of any peace with Demetrius: they did then, upon Lachares' fleeing, presently open the gates next unto Demetrius' camp, and sent ambassadors unto him, not looking for any grace or peace, but because necessity drove them to it.

Part Two

During this so hard and strait siege, there fell out many wonderful and strange things: but among others, this one is of special note. It is reported that a father and the son sitting in their house, void of all hope of life: there fell a dead rat *[Dryden: mouse]* before them from the top of the house, and that the father and son fought who should have it to eat. Moreover, that at the selfsame siege the philosopher **Epicurus** maintained himself and his scholars, by giving them **a proportion** of beans every day, by the which they lived.

In this condition was the city when Demetrius made his entrance and issued a proclamation that all the inhabitants should assemble in the theater; which being done, he drew up his soldiers at the back of the stage, occupied the stage itself with his guards, and presently coming in himself by the actors' passages, when the people's **consternation** had risen to its height, with his first words he put an end to it.

For he did not fashion his oration with a hasty angry voice, neither did he use any sharp or bitter words: but only after he had courteously told them their faults and discourtesy towards him, he said he forgave them, and that he would be their friend again: and furthermore, he caused ten million bushels of wheat to be given unto them, and appointed as magistrates persons acceptable to the people.

Then Dromoclides the orator, seeing that the people gave out great shouts of joy in the praise of Demetrius, and that the orators daily contended **in the pulpit for orations**, who should exceed the others in **preferring** new honours for Demetrius: he caused an order to be made, that the havens of Piraeus and Munichia should be put into Demetrius' hands, to use at his pleasure. This was passed accordingly, and Demetrius, of his own motion, added a third garrison *[omission]* as a precaution against any new restiveness on the part of the people, **which might give him the trouble of quitting his other enterprises**.

Part Three

He had not long been master of Athens before he had formed designs against **Lacedaemon**; of which **Archidamus**, the king, being advertised, came out and met him, but he was overthrown in a battle near Mantinea; after which Demetrius entered **Laconia**, and, in a second battle near **Sparta** itself, defeated him [Archidamus] again with the loss of two hundred Lacedaemonians slain, and five hundred taken prisoners. And now it was almost impossible for the city, which hitherto had never been captured, to escape his arms.

But certainly there never was any king upon whom Fortune made such short turns, nor any other life or story so filled with her swift and surprising changes, over and over again, from small things to great, from splendour back to humiliation and from utter weakness once more to power and might *[omission]*. Now again when Demetrius' affairs prospered so well, and that he was likely to recover a great force and kingdom: news was brought to him, first, that Lysimachus had taken all his towns from him, which he held in Asia; and on the other side, that Ptolemy had reduced all Cyprus with the exception of Salamis, and that in Salamis **his mother and children** were shut up and close besieged *[omission]*.

The same fortune that drew him off with these disastrous tidings from Sparta, in a moment after opened upon him a new and wonderful prospect, of the following kind. Cassander, king of Macedon, dying, and his eldest son, Philip, who succeeded him, not long surviving his father, the two younger brothers fell at variance concerning the succession. And Antipater having murdered his mother Thessalonica, Alexander, the younger brother, called in to aid him Demetrius and

Pyrrhus, the one out of the realm of Epirus, and the other out of Peloponnesus.

Pyrrhus arrived first, and, taking in **recompense for his succour** a large slice of Macedonia, had made Alexander begin to be aware that he had brought upon himself a dangerous neighbour. And, that he might not run a yet worse hazard from Demetrius, whose power and reputation were so great, the young man hurried away to meet him at **Dium**, whither he, who on receiving his letter, had set out on his march, was now come. And, offering his greetings and grateful acknowledgements, he at the same time informed him that his affairs no longer required the presence of his ally; thereupon he invited him to supper.

There were not wanting some feelings of suspicion on either side already. So it chanced that as Demetrius went to Alexander's lodging where the feast was prepared: there came one to him to tell him of an ambush that was laid for him, and how they had determined to kill him when he should think to be merry at the banquet. But Demetrius was nothing abashed at the news, and only went a little softlier, not making such haste as he did before, and in the meantime sent to command his captains to arm their men, and to have them in readiness: and willed his gentlemen and all the rest of his officers that were about him, (which were a greater number by many than those of Alexander's side) every man of them to go in with him into the hall, and to tarry there till he rose from the table. Thus Alexander's servants, finding themselves overpowered, had not courage to attempt anything. Furthermore, Demetrius feigning that he was not well at ease at that time to make merry, he went immediately out of the hall, and the next morning determined to depart, making him believe that he had certain news brought him of great importance: and prayed Alexander to pardon him, that he could no longer keep him company, for that he was driven of necessity to depart from him, and that another time they would meet together, with better leisure and liberty.

Narration and Discussion

Try to chart the "ups and downs" of Demetrius' life and career at this time. What were the times in which he showed wisdom and good leadership? When did he not do so well?

Why did Alexander change his mind about accepting help from Demetrius? Describe the cat-and-mouse game that they played. How do you think this will end?

Creative narration #1: Dramatize the scene in which Demetrius addressed the people of Athens after the siege.

Creative narration #2: Continue the "family history project."

Lesson Eight

Introduction

Demetrius, like a game player collecting up properties, became ruler of Athens, and king of both Macedon and Thessaly. However, as in a game, the tables could easily be turned.

Vocabulary

assail: attack

orations: speeches

clemency: mercy, forgiveness

two furlongs: a furlong was equivalent to 220 yards (201 m)

heat and contentiousness: anger, spite

seditious: rebellious

animosity: resentment, hatred

People

Cleonymus of Sparta: a member of the Spartan royal family with a rather complicated career history. The Spartans sent him to Boeotia to help defend it against Demetrius.

Hieronymus, the historian: the writings of Hieronymus may have been one of Plutarch's sources for this *Life*

Pyrrhus: see introductory notes

Pantauchus: a Macedonian general

Historic Occasions

294 B.C.: Demetrius' murder of Alexander of Macedon

294 B.C.: Demetrius' actions in Sparta

292-291 B.C.: The events described here in Boeotia

292 B.C.: Pyrrhus invaded Thessaly, but withdrew after a counterattack by Demetrius

291 B.C.: Lanassa left her husband Pyrrhus for Demetrius

On the Map

Thessaly: a region of Greece; its capital was **Larissa**

Boeotia (Boeotians): another region of Greece; its capital was **Thebes**

Thespiae (Thespians): a city which belonged to the Boeotian League

Thrace: a region now split among Greece, Bulgaria, and Turkey

Thermopylae: a narrow coastal passage into Greece

Delphi: among other things, it was the traditional site of the games

Reading

Part One

Alexander was very glad to see that Demetrius went his way out of Macedon not offended, but of his own goodwill; and proceeded to accompany him into **Thessaly**. But when they came to **Lariss**a, new invitations passed between them, new professions of goodwill, covering new conspiracies; by which Alexander put himself into the power of Demetrius. For as he did not like to use precautions on his own part, for fear Demetrius should take the hint to use them on his, the very thing he meant to do was first done to him. He accepted an invitation, and came to Demetrius's quarters; and when Demetrius, while they were still supping, rose from the table and went forth, the young man rose also, and followed him to the door, where Demetrius, as he passed through, only said to the guards, "Kill him that follows me," and went on; and Alexander was at once despatched by them, together with such of his friends as endeavoured to come to his rescue, one of whom, before he died, said, "You have been one day too quick for us."

All that night was (as may be supposed) full of uproar and tumult. Howbeit, the next morning the Macedonians being marvellously troubled and afraid of Demetrius' great power; when they saw that no man came to **assail** them, but that Demetrius in contrary manner sent unto them to tell them that he would speak with them, and deliver them reason for that he had done; then they all began to be bold again, and willingly gave him audience. Now Demetrius needed not to use many words, nor to make any long **orations**, to win them unto him: for, because they hated Antipater for his murder of his mother; and because they had no better man to prefer, they easily chose Demetrius king of Macedon, and thereupon brought him back into Macedon, to take possession of the kingdom.

And the Macedonians at home, who had not forgotten or forgiven the wicked deeds committed by Cassander on the family of Alexander, were far from sorry at the change. Any kind recollections that still might subsist of the plain and simple rule of the first Antipater went also to the benefit of Demetrius, whose wife was Phila, Antipater's daughter; and his son by her, a boy already old enough to be serving in the army with his father, was the natural successor to the government.

To add to this unexpected good fortune, news arrived that Ptolemy had dismissed his [Demetrius'] mother and children, bestowing upon them presents and honours; and also that his daughter Stratonice, whom he had married to Seleucus, was remarried to Antiochus, the son of Seleucus, and proclaimed Queen of Upper Asia.

[Omission for length and content. Note: why did Seleucus allow his wife to be married to his son, an unusual act even in his time and culture? Short version: the son was so lovesick that Seleucus took pity on him.]

Part Two

Having obtained the crown of Macedon, Demetrius presently became master of Thessaly, also. And holding the greatest part of Peloponnesus, and, on this side of the Isthmus, the cities of Megara and Athens, he now turned his arms against the **Boeotians**. They at first were willing to make peace with him. But **Cleonymus of Sparta** having ventured with some troops to their assistance, and having made his way into **Thebes**, and Pisis the Thespian, who was their first man in power and reputation, animating them to make a brave resistance, they broke off the treaty.

No sooner, however, had Demetrius begun to approach the walls with his engines, by Cleonymus in affright secretly withdrew; and the Boeotians, finding themselves abandoned, made their submission. Demetrius placed a garrison in charge of their towns, and, having raised a large sum of money from them, he placed **Hieronymus, the historian**, in the office of governor and military commander over them, and was thought on the whole to have shown great **clemency**, more particularly to Pisis, to whom he did no hurt, but spoke with him courteously and kindly, and made him chief magistrate of **Thespiae**.

Part Three

Not long after, Lysimachus by chance was taken prisoner by another prince called Dromichaetes; and Demetrius went off instantly in the hopes of possessing himself of **Thrace**, thus left without a king. Upon this the Boeotians revolted again, and news also came that Lysimachus had regained his liberty. Then he [Demetrius] returned back with all speed, marvellously offended with the Boeotians, whom he found already discomfited in battle by his son Antigonus (#2); and he went again to lay siege to the city of Thebes, being the chief city of all that province of Boeotia.

But understanding that Pyrrhus had made an incursion into Thessaly, and that he was advanced as far as **Thermopylae**, leaving

Antigonus to continue the siege, he marched with the rest of his army to oppose this enemy. Pyrrhus, however, made a quick retreat. So, leaving ten thousand foot and a thousand horse for the protection of Thessaly, he returned to the siege of Thebes, and there brought up his famous City-Taker to the attack; which, however, was so labouriously and so slowly moved on account of its bulk and heaviness, that in two months it did not advance **two furlongs**.

In the meantime the citizens made a stout defense, and Demetrius, out of **heat and contentiousness** very often, more than upon any necessity, sent his soldiers into danger; until at last Antigonus, observing how many men were losing their lives, said to him, "Why, my father, do we go on letting the men be wasted in this way without any need of it?" But Demetrius, in a great passion, interrupted him, "And you, good sir, why do you afflict yourself for the matter? Will dead men come to you for rations?" But that the soldiers might see that he valued his own life at no dearer rate than theirs, he fought with them freely, and was wounded with a javelin through his neck, which put him into great hazard of his life. But, notwithstanding, he continued the siege, and in conclusion took the town again.

And after his entrance, when the citizens were in fear and trembling, and expected all the severities which an incensed conqueror could inflict, he only put to death thirteen and banished some few others, pardoning all the rest. Thus the city of Thebes, which had not yet been ten years restored, in that short space was twice besieged and taken.

Shortly after, the Festival of the Pythian Apollo was to be celebrated, and the Aetolians having blocked up all the passages to **Delphi**, Demetrius held the games and celebrated the feast at Athens, alleging there was great reason those honours should paid in that place, Apollo being the paternal god of the Athenian people, and the reputed first founder of their race.

From thence he returned into Macedon, and knowing that it was against his nature to live idly and in peace, and seeing on the other side also that the Macedonians did him more service, and were more obedient to him in wars, and that in time of peace they grew **seditious**, full of vanity and quarrel: he went to make war with the Aetolians, and after he had spoiled and destroyed their country, he left **Pantauchus** as his lieutenant there, with a great part of his army.

Demetrius himself went in the meantime with the rest of his army against Pyrrhus: and Pyrrhus also against him, but they missed of meeting each with other. But whilst Demetrius entered Epirus, and laid all waste before him, Pyrrhus fell upon Pantauchus, and in a battle in which the two commanders met in person and wounded each other, he gained the victory, and took five thousand prisoners, besides great numbers slain in the field.

The worst thing, however, for Demetrius was that Pyrrhus had excited less **animosity** as an enemy than admiration as a brave man. His taking so large a part with his own hand in the battle had gained him the greatest name and glory among the Macedonians.

Narration and Discussion

Demetrius said to his son, "What needest thou to care? Is there any corn to be distributed to those that are dead?" (North's translation). Why might he have said this? Did his actions afterwards speak louder than his words?

Creative narration #1: Write or act out a conversation between two Macedonians, one who has become a fan of Pyrrhus, and the other defending Demetrius.

Creative narration #2: Continue the "family history project."

For further thought: Is it true that people are more easily ruled in wartime than in peace?

Lesson Nine

Introduction

Demetrius now had a true rival for power: Pyrrhus, whom, it was believed, carried on the greatness of Alexander. Demetrius' kingly robes no longer seemed to impress the people, and neither did his arrogance. But he was not willing to give up the throne of Macedonia—his "home turf"—without a fight.

Vocabulary

personate: imitate

when his reverse overtook him: when he lost his kingdom

envoys: ambassadors

after the Laconian manner: in few words

in some apparent fit of a more popular and acceptable temper: wanting to appear more friendly to the people

written petitions: formal requests to have their cases heard

levying: gathering

on the stocks: being built

execrations: denunciations, curses

rifle: rob, loot

Historic Occasions

289 B.C.: After winning the battle against Macedonian forces led by Pantauchus, the Epirots returned to their own country (as did the Macedonians). Later the same year, though, Demetrius became ill, and Pyrrhus took advantage of the situation to invade Macedonia.

289-288 B.C.: Demetrius made peace with Pyrrhus but was already making plans against Asia.

288 B.C: Lysimachus and Pyrrhus became co-rulers of Macedon.

On the Map

Pella: the capital city of Macedonia

Edessa: another important city of Macedonia

Beroea (also Veria, Veroia, or Berea): a city of Macedonia, mentioned in Acts 17.

Reading

Part One

Now many of the Macedonians began to say that Pyrrhus was the only king in whom there was any likeness to be seen of the great Alexander's courage; the other kings, and particularly Demetrius, did nothing but **personate** him, like actors on a stage, in his pomp and outward majesty.

And Demetrius truly was a perfect play and pageant, with his robes and diadems, his gold-edged purple and his hats with double streamers, his very shoes being of the richest purple felt, embroidered over in gold. One robe in particular, a most superb piece of work, was long in the loom in preparation for him, in which was to be wrought the representation of the universe and the celestial bodies. This, left unfinished **when his reverse overtook him**, not any one of the kings of Macedon, his successors, though divers of them proud and arrogant enough, ever presumed to use.

But it was not this theatric pomp alone which disgusted the Macedonians, but his profuse and luxurious way of living; and, above all, the difficulty of speaking with him or of obtaining access to his presence. For either he would not be seen at all, or, if he did give audience, he was violent and overbearing. Thus he made the **envoys** of the Athenians, to whom yet he was more attentive than to all the other Grecians, wait two whole years before they could obtain a hearing. Another time also he was offended, because the Lacedaemonians had sent but one man only as ambassador unto him, taking it that they had done it in despite of him. And so did the ambassador of the Lacedaemonians answer him very gallantly, **after the Laconian manner**. For when Demetrius asked him, "How chanceth it that the Lacedaemonians do send but one man unto me?" "No more but one," said he, "O king, unto one."

Once when, **in some apparent fit of a more popular and acceptable temper,** he was riding abroad, a number of people came up and presented their **written petitions**. He courteously received all these, and put them up in the skirt of his cloak, while the poor people were overjoyed, and followed him close. But when he came upon the bridge of the river Axius, shaking out his cloak, he threw all into the river. This went to the hearts of the Macedonians, who then thought they were no more governed by a king, but oppressed by a tyrant. They called to mind what some of them had seen, and others had heard related of King Philip's unambitious and open, accessible manners. One day when an old woman had assailed him [Philip] several times in the road, and importuned him to hear her after he had told her he had no tie, "If so," cried she, "you have no time to be a king." And this reprimand so stung the king that, after thinking of it awhile, he went back into the house, and setting all other matters apart, for several days together he did nothing else but receive, beginning with the old woman, the complaints of all that would come. And to do justice, truly enough, might well be called a king's first business *[omission]*.

Part Two

Demetrius fell into a great and dangerous sickness in the city of **Pella**, and during this time Pyrrhus pretty nearly overran all Macedon, and advanced as far as the city of **Edessa**. On recovering his health, he [Demetrius] quickly drove him out, and came to terms with him, being desirous not to employ his time in a string of petty local conflicts with a neighbour, when all his thoughts were fixed upon another design. This was no less than to endeavour the recovery of the whole empire which his father had possessed, and his preparations were suitable to his hopes and the greatness of the enterprise. He had arranged for the **levying** of ninety-eight thousand foot and nearly twelve thousand horse; and he had a fleet of five hundred galleys **on the stocks**, some building at Athens, others at Corinth and Chalcis, and in the neighbourhood of Pella. And he himself was passing evermore from one to another of these places, to give his directions and his assistance to the plans, while all that saw were amazed, not so much at the number, as at the magnitude of the works. Hitherto, there had never been seen a galley with fifteen or sixteen ranges of oars.

[omitted for length: comparison to a later, even larger Egyptian ship]

These mighty preparations against Asia, the like of which had not been made since Alexander first invaded it, united Seleucus, Ptolemy, and Lysimachus in a confederacy for their defense. They also despatched ambassadors to Pyrrhus, to persuade him to make a diversion by attacking Macedonia; he need not think there was any validity in a treaty which Demetrius had concluded, not as an engagement to be at peace with him, but as a means for enabling himself to make war first upon the enemy of his choice.

Part Three

So when Pyrrhus accepted their proposals, Demetrius, still in the midst of his preparations, was encompassed with war on all sides. Ptolemy, with a mighty navy, invaded Greece; Lysimachus entered Macedonia upon the side of Thrace, and Pyrrhus, from the Epirot border, both of them spoiling and wasting the country.

Demetrius, leaving his son to look after Greece, marched to the relief of Macedon, and first of all to oppose Lysimachus. On his way, he received the news that Pyrrhus had taken the city of **Beroea**; and this news being blown abroad amongst the Macedonians, all Demetrius' doings were turned topsy turvy. The camp was filled with lamentations and tears, anger and **execrations** on Demetrius; they would stay no longer, they would march off, as they said, to take care of their country, friends, and families; but in reality the intention was to yield themselves unto Lysimachus. Demetrius, therefore, thought it his business to keep them as far away as he could from Lysimachus, who was their own countryman, and for Alexander's sake kindly looked upon by many; they would be ready to fight with Pyrrhus, a newcomer and a foreigner, whom they could hardly prefer to himself.

But there his judgement failed him. For when he advanced and pitched his camp near, the old admiration for Pyrrhus's gallantry in arms revived again; and as they had been used from time immemorial to suppose that the best king was he that was the bravest soldier, so now they were also told of his [Pyrrhus'] generous usage of his prisoners; and, in short, they were eager to have anyone in the place of Demetrius, and well pleased that the man should be Pyrrhus.

At first, some straggling parties only deserted; but in a little time the whole army broke out into a universal mutiny, insomuch that at last some of them went up and told him openly that if he consulted his own safety he were best to make haste to be gone, for that the Macedonians were resolved no longer to hazard their lives for the satisfaction of his luxury and pleasure. And this was thought fair and moderate language, compared with the fierceness of the rest.

So Demetrius went into his tent, and cast a black cloak about his face, instead of his rich and stately cloak he was wont to wear: not like unto a king, but like a common player when the play is done, and then secretly stole away.

When this was known in the camp, many of his soldiers ran to his tent to **rifle** it, and every man took such hold of it to have his part, that they tore it in pieces, and drew their swords to fight for it. But Pyrrhus, coming immediately took possession of the camp without a blow, after which he, with Lysimachus, parted the realm of Macedon betwixt them, after Demetrius had securely held it just seven years.

Narration and Discussion

Demetrius had great plans and built wonderful warships. How did his "mighty preparations" now work against him?

Creative narration #1: As an interviewer, talk to people on the streets of Macedonia, either before or after the news that the kingdom had fallen to Pyrrhus and Lysimachus. What did they have to say about Demetrius?

Creative narration #2: Continue the "family history project." How might Antigonus (#2) have viewed his father's overthrow?

Lesson Ten

Introduction

Demetrius was, by this point, "the most miserable king." But, being Demetrius, he always seemed to have a plan for recovery; and this one began with Athens. He began a siege there, and was then talked out of it, perhaps distracted by the promise of better territory waiting for him in Asia. Fortune, however, seemed to be deserting him on this expedition.

Vocabulary

calamity: disaster

archons: Athenian magistrates

affianced: engaged

straitened him much in his forage: made it hard for him to get food and supplies

to gauge the ford: to judge the depth and conditions of the river crossing

pass their jests: make jokes

Oedipus: *Oedipus Rex*, a tragedy by Sophocles

in their extreme necessity: in their dire need

victuals: food

People

Crates the philosopher: Crates of Thebes, who was likely a student of Stilpo (**Lesson Two**)

Agathocles, the son of Lysimachus: a prince who would have been, it was assumed, Lysimachus' heir; but because of family intrigues and strife, he was put to death soon afterwards on suspicion of treason.

Historic Occasions

288 B.C.: Demetrius fled to Cassandrea

288/287 B.C.: Demetrius' wife **Phila killed herself with poison**

c.287 B.C.: Demetrius married Ptolemais

287 B.C.: Demetrius besieged Athens

287/286 B.C.: Demetrius left Antigonus (#2) in charge of the war in Greece, and seized power in **Caria and Lydia**, provinces of

Lysimachus; he also captured **Sardis**

286 B.C.: Demetrius and his army retreated to eastern Asia Minor

286/285 B.C.: Demetrius requested a small mountain territory for himself

On the Map

Cassandrea or **Cassandreia:** an important city in Macedonia

Asia: This does not refer to the continent as we know it, but to **Anatolia** or **Asia Minor**, which included the regions of **Caria** and **Lydia. Lydia's** capital city was **Sardis.**

Miletus: a city on the west coast of **Anatolia**

Armenia: at that time, a country of western **Asia**

Media (Medes): a region now part of northwestern Iran

Tarsus: a city in Cilicia, known as the birthplace of St. Paul

Mount Taurus: The Taurus Mountains are a range across the southern coast of **Asia Minor.**

Cataonia: a region of **Cappadocia**, in **Asia Minor**

Reading

Part One

Now Demetrius being thus miserably overthrown, and turned out of all his realm: he fled unto the city of **Cassandrea**. His wife Phila, in the passion of her grief, could not endure to see her hapless husband reduced to the condition of a private and banished man. She refused to entertain any further hope, and resolving to quit a fortune which was never permanent except for **calamity**, took poison and died.

Demetrius, determining still to hold on by the wreck, went off to Greece, and collected his friends and officers there.

[omitted: thoughts about the rising and falling of one's fortunes]

Part Two

Now when he began to have some hope again, and (as it were) entered into the great highway of kings, he began once more to have about him the body and form of empire.

The Thebans received back, as his gift, their ancient constitution.

The Athenians had deserted him. They displaced Diphilus, who was that year the priest of the two Tutelar Deities, and restored the **archons**, as of old, to mark the year; and on hearing that Demetrius was not so weak as they had expected, they sent into Macedonia to beg the protection of Pyrrhus. Demetrius, in anger, marched to Athens, and laid close siege to the city.

In this distress they sent out to him **Crates the philosopher**, a person of authority and reputation, who succeeded so far that, what with his entreaties and the solid reasons which he offered, Demetrius was persuaded to raise the siege; and, collecting all his ships, he embarked a force of eleven thousand men with cavalry, and sailed away to **Asia**, to **Caria** and **Lydia**, to take those provinces from Lysimachus.

Arriving at **Miletus**, he was met there by Eurydice, the sister of Phila, who brought along with her Ptolemais, one of her daughters by King Ptolemy, who had before been **affianced** to Demetrius. So he married Ptolemais there, with the goodwill and consent of her mother Eurydice.

Part Three

Immediately after, he proceeded to carry out his project, and was so fortunate in the beginning that many cities revolted to him; others, as particularly **Sardis**, he took by force; and some generals of Lysimachus, also, came over to him with troops and money.

But when **Agathocles, the son of Lysimachus**, arrived with an army, he retreated into Phrygia, with an intention to pass into **Armenia**, believing that, if he could once plant his foot in Armenia, he might set **Media** in revolt, and gain a position in Upper Asia, where a fugitive commander might find a hundred ways of evasion and escape.

Agathocles followed him very near, and many skirmishes and

conflicts occurred, in which Demetrius had still the advantage; but Agathocles **straitened him much in his forage**, and his men showed a great dislike to his purpose, which they suspected, of carrying them far away into Armenia and Media. The famine daily increased more and more in his army, and it chanced besides, that missing his way, and failing **to gauge the ford** well as he passed over the river of Lycus, the fury and force of the river carried his men down the stream, and drowned a great number of them.

Still, however, they could **pass their jests**, and one of them fixed upon Demetrius's tent-door a paper with the first verse, slightly altered, of the *Oedipus*:--

Child of the blind old man, Antigonus,

Into what country are you bringing us?

The plague began also in the midst of this famine, (a common thing, and almost a matter of necessity, it should so be) because that men being driven to need and necessity, do frame themselves to eat all that comes to hand: whereupon he was driven to bring back those few men that remained, having lost of all sorts (good and bad) not so few as eight thousand, fully told.

Part Four

With the rest of his men, Demetrius retreated and came to **Tarsus**. And because that city was within the dominions of Seleucus, he was anxious to prevent any plundering, and wished to give no sort of offense to Seleucus.

But when he perceived it was impossible to restrain the soldiers **in their extreme necessity**, Agathocles also having blocked up all the avenues of Mount Taurus, he wrote a letter to Seleucus, bewailing first all his own sad fortunes, and proceeding with entreaties and supplications for some compassion on his part towards one nearly connected with him, who was fallen into such calamities as might extort tenderness and pity from his very enemies.

These letters somewhat softened Seleucus' heart, insomuch that he wrote to his governors and lieutenants of those parts to furnish Demetrius' person with all things needful for a prince's house, and **victuals** sufficient to maintain his men.

But Patrocles, a person whose judgment was greatly valued, and who was a friend highly trusted by Seleucus, pointed out to him that the expense of maintaining such a body of soldiers was the least important consideration, but that it was contrary to all policy to let Demetrius stay in the country, since he, of all the kings of his time, was the most violent, and most addicted to daring enterprises; and he was now in a condition which might tempt persons of the greatest temper and moderation to unlawful and desperate attempts.

Seleucus, being moved with these persuasions, presently took his journey into Cilicia with a great army. Demetrius being astonished with this sudden change, and dreading so great an army, got him to the strongest places of **Mount Taurus**.

From there he went envoys to Seleucus, to request from him that he would permit him the liberty to settle with his army somewhere among the independent barbarian tribes, where he might be able to make himself a petty king, and end his life without further travel and hardship; or, if he refused him this, at any rate to give his troops food during the winter, and not expose him in this distressed and naked condition to the fury of his enemies. But Seleucus, mistrusting his demands, sent unto him that he should winter if he thought good, two months, but no more, **in Cataonia**, provided he gave him the chiefest of his friends for hostages. Howbeit, in the meantime, Seleucus stopped up all the ways and passages going from thence into Syria.

Narration and Discussion

Was Demetrius still showing good judgment as a military leader? How did he handle the problems of sickness and lack of food in the camp?

Creative narration #1: Write some diary entries or a letter home by one of Demetrius' soldiers.

Creative narration #2: Continue the "family history project."

Creative narration #3 (for older students): Write a Shakespearian monologue for Demetrius, trying to decide whether to beg for help from Seleucus.

Lesson Eleven

Introduction

After a chase through **Cyrrhestica**, Seleucus caught up with Demetrius and put him under house arrest. But what was he then to do with him? He could kill him, of course. But if he let Demetrius go, perhaps with conditions, he could remind him forever of how kind he had been. This was definitely a difficult position to be in.

Vocabulary

armed carts with scythes: chariots with blades attached

elated: delighted, happy

putting on his boots: North says "putting on his hose"

mercenary soldiers: hired soldiers, often foreigners

vicissitudes: sudden changes of fortune

surrender at discretion: surrender unconditionally

pavilion: tent

signet: a ring used as identification

protracted the time: delayed things

Historic Occasions

285 B.C.: Demetrius fought with Seleucus in Syria, but became ill, and essentially surrendered himself

284 B.C.: Lysimachus had his son Agathocles put to death on suspicion of treason

On the Map

Cyrrhestica: a district of **Syria**, located east of **Amanus** (a mountain range also called the **Nur Mountains**)

Caunus (Kaumos): a seaport city in Anatolia

Chersonesus of Syria or Syrian Chersonese: The exact location of this is undetermined, but it is believed to be near **Antioch**, a city founded by Seleucus near the **Orontes River**

Reading

Part One

So that Demetrius, who saw himself thus, like a wild beast, encompassed on all sides, was driven to trust to his own strength. Thereupon he overran the country thereabouts, and as often as it was his chance to have any skirmish or conflict with Seleucus, he had ever the better of him: and when they drove the **armed carts with scythes** against him, he overcame them, and put the rest to flight. Then, expelling the troops that were in guard of the mountain passes, made himself master of the roads leading into Syria. And now, **elated** himself, and finding his soldiers also animated by these successes, he was resolved to push ahead, and to have one deciding blow for the empire with Seleucus; who indeed was in considerable anxiety and distress, being averse to any assistance from Lysimachus, whom he both mistrusted and feared; and shrinking from a battle with Demetrius, whose desperation he knew, and whose fortune he had so often seen suddenly pass from the lowest to the highest.

But in the meanwhile, Demetrius fell into a great sickness, the which brought his body very weak and low, and had almost utterly overthrown his affairs. His men deserted to the enemy, or dispersed. At last, after forty days, he began to be so far recovered as to be able to rally his remaining forces, and marched as if he directly designed for Cilicia; but in the night, raising his camp without sound of trumpet, he took a countermarch, and, passing the mountain **Amanus**, he ravaged all the lower country as far as **Cyrrhestica**.

But Seleucus followed him, and camped close by. Thereupon

Demetrius suddenly armed his men, and went out by night to assault Seleucus, and to take him sleeping when he mistrusted nothing. So that Seleucus knew nothing of his stealing on him but late enough, until that certain traitors of Demetrius' camp that fled before, went quickly to advertise him, finding him asleep, and brought him news of the danger he was in. Then Seleucus in amazement and fear withal, got up, and sounded the alarm: and as he was **putting on his boots** to mount his horse, he cried out (speaking to his friends and familiars about him), "We have now a cruel and dangerous beast to deal with."

But Demetrius, by the noise he heard in the camp, finding they had taken the alarm, drew off his troops in haste.

Part Two

The next morning by break of day, Seleucus went and offered him battle. Demetrius prepared himself to join with him, and having given one of his faithful friends the leading of one of the wings of his army, himself led the other, and overthrew some of his enemies on his side. But Seleucus, lighting from his horse, pulling off his helmet, and taking a target, advanced to the foremost ranks of the **mercenary soldiers**, and, showing them who he was, bade them come over and join him, telling them that it was for their sakes only that he had so long forborne coming to extremities. And thereupon without a blow more, they saluted Seleucus as their king and passed over.

Demetrius, who felt that this was his last change of fortune, and that he had no more **vicissitudes** to expect, fled to the passes of Amanus, where, with a very few friends and followers, he threw himself into a dense forest, and there waited for the night, purposing, if possible to make his escape towards **Caunus**, where he hoped to find his shipping ready to transport him. But upon inquiry, finding that they had not provisions even for that one day, he began then to devise some other way. At length, one of his familiar friends, Sosigenes, came unto him, that had four hundred pieces of gold about him. So hoping that with the same money he might flee to the sea, they took their way by night directly, to the top of the mountain.

But, perceiving by the fires that the enemies had occupied them, he gave up all thought of that road, and retreated to his old station in the wood, but not with all his men; for some had deserted, nor were those that remained as willing as they had been. So, one among the rest took upon him to say that there was no other way to escape, but to put Demetrius into Seleucus' hands. Demetrius therewithal drew out his sword, and would have slain himself: but his friends about him would not suffer him, but persuading him to do as had been said. So at last he gave way, and sent to Seleucus, to **surrender himself at discretion.**

Part Three

Seleucus was so joyful of the news, that he said it was not Demetrius' good fortune that saved him, but his own, which had added to his other honours the opportunity of showing his clemency and generosity. And forthwith he gave order to his officers of household, and commanded them to set up his richest **pavilion**, and to prepare all things meet to receive him honourably.

There was one Appolonides, a gentleman in Seleucus' court, who sometime had been very familiar with Demetrius. Seleucus sent him immediately unto Demetrius, to will him to be of good cheer, and not to be afraid to come to the king his master, for he should find him his very good friend. No sooner was this message known, but the courtiers and officers, some few at first, and afterwards almost the whole of them, thinking Demetrius would presently become of great power with the king, hurried off, vying who should be foremost to pay him their respects. But hereby they turned Seleucus' pity into envy, and gave occasion also to Demetrius' enemies and spiteful men, to turn the king's bountiful good nature from him. For they put into his head many doubts and dangers, saying, that certainly so soon as the soldiers saw him, there would grow great stir and change in their camp.

And therefore, shortly after that Apollonides was come unto Demetrius, being glad to bring him these good news, and as others also followed him one after another, bringing him some good words from Seleucus, and that Demetrius himself after so great an overthrow (although that before he thought it a shameful part of him to have yielded his body into his enemy's hands) changed his mind at that time, and began then to grow bold, and to have good hope to recover his state again: behold, there came one of Seleucus' captains, called Pausanias, accompanied with a thousand footmen and horsemen in all, who compassed in Demetrius with them, and made the rest depart that were come unto him before, having charge given him not to bring him to the court, but to convey him into **Chersonesus of Syria**, whither he was brought, and ever after had a strong garrison about him to keep him.

But otherwise, Seleucus sent him officers, money, and all things else meet for a prince's house: and his ordinary fare was so delicate, that he could wish for no more than he had. And furthermore, he had places of liberty and pleasure appointed him, both to ride his horse in, and also pleasant walks, and goodly arbours to walk or sit in, and fine parks full of beasts where he might hunt: moreover, the king allowed his own household servants that followed him when he fled, to remain with him if they would. And furthermore, there daily came someone or other unto him from Seleucus, to comfort him, and to put him in hope that so soon as Antiochus and Stratonice were come, they would make some good agreement and peace between them.

Demetrius, however, finding himself in this condition, sent letters to those who were with his son, and to his captains and friends at Athens and Corinth, that they should give no manner of credit to any letters written to them in his name, though they were sealed with his own **signet**, but that, looking upon him as if he were already dead, they should maintain the cities and whatever was left of his power for Antigonus, as his successor.

Antigonus received the news of his father's captivity with great sorrow. He put himself into mourning and wrote letters to the rest of the kings, and to Seleucus himself, making entreaties, and offering not only to surrender whatever they had left, but himself to be a hostage for his father. Many cities also and princes joined in interceding for him; only Lysimachus sent and offered a large sum of money to Seleucus to take away his life. But he, who had always shown his aversion to Lysimachus before, thought him only the greater barbarian and monster for it. Nevertheless, he still **protracted the time**, reserving the favour, as he professed, for the intercession of Antiochus and Stratonice.

Narration and Discussion

At the beginning of this passage, why did Seleucus not want to fight against Demetrius? What changed things?

When Demetrius finally surrendered to Seleucus, why was Seleucus so lenient with him? Should he have taken Lysimachus' advice and put him to death?

Creative narration #1: Dramatize any part of this passage.

Creative narration #2: Continue the "family history project."

For further thought: Plutarch makes this interesting comment: "So that Demetrius, who saw himself thus, like a wild beast, encompassed on all sides, was driven to trust to his own strength." He seems to imply that this was not a good thing. What or who else might Demetrius have trusted?

For older students: Can you think of any other stories of people suddenly having their enemy in their hands, but not knowing what to do with them? (One example: Elizabeth I and Mary Queen of Scots.)

Lesson Twelve and Examination Questions

Introduction

Seleucus was relieved of the need to make a decision about Demetrius, as he died of more-or-less natural causes. His death seemed to cause a surprising amount of sorrow…or was it just for show? You will have to decide for yourself.

Vocabulary

gross: overweight

he himself also did much repent him: he was very sorry

cadences: beat, rhythm

People

Perseus (212-166 B.C.): the last king of Macedon

Historic Occasions

283 B.C.: Death of Demetrius

239 B.C.: Death of Antigonus II Gonatas (Demetrius' son)

On the Map

Iolcus: a town of ancient Thessaly, whose inhabitants became part of Demetrius' new city there

Reading

Part One

Now for Demetrius, as he from the beginning patiently took his hard fortune, so did he daily more and more forget the misery he was in. For first of all, he gave himself to riding and hunting, as far as the place gave him liberty. Then by little and little he grew to be very **gross**, and to give over such pastimes, and therewithal he took to dice and drinking, in which he passed most of his time, whether it were to escape the thoughts of his present condition, with which he was haunted when sober, and to drown reflection in drunkenness, or that he acknowledged to himself that this was the real happy life he had long desired and wished for, and had foolishly let himself be seduced away from it by a senseless and vain ambition , which had only brought trouble to others; that highest good which he had thought to obtain by arms and fleets and soldiers he had now discovered unexpectedly in idleness, leisure, and repose. As, indeed, what other end or period is there of all the wars and dangers which hapless princes run into, whose misery and folly it is, not merely that they make luxury and pleasure, instead of virtue and excellence, the object of their lives, but that they do not so much as know where this luxury and pleasure are to be found?

Part Two

So, Demetrius after he had been shut up in Chersonesus three years together, by ease, grossness, and drunkenness, fell sick of a disease whereof he died, when he was four and fifty years old. Therefore was Seleucus greatly blamed, and **he himself also did much repent him** that he so suspected him as he did, and that he had let himself be so much outdone by the barbarian Dromichaetes of Thrace, who had shown so much humanity and such a kingly temper in his treatment of his prisoner Lysimachus.

But yet there was some tragical pomp in the order of his funeral. For his son Antigonus understanding that they brought him the ashes of his body, he took sea with all his ships, and went to meet them, to receive them in the isles. They were there presented to him in a golden urn, which he placed in his largest admiral galley. So, all the cities and towns whereby they passed, or harboured, some of them did put garlands of flowers about the funeral urn, others also sent a number of men thither in mourning apparel, to accompany and honour the convoy, to the very solemnity of his funerals.

In this sort sailed all the whole fleet towards the city of Corinth, the urn being plainly seen far off, standing on the top of the admiral galley: all the place about it being hanged about with purple, and over it, the diadem or royal band, and about it also were goodly young men armed, to receive it at landing. Xenophantus, the most famous musician of the day, played on the flute his most solemn measure, to which the rowers, as the ship came in, made loud response, their oars, like the funeral beating of the breast, keeping time with the **cadences** of the music.

But that which most made the people of Corinth to weep and lament, which ran to the pier, and all alongst the shoreside to see it: was Antigonus (#2), whom they saw all beblubbered with tears, appareled as a mourner in blacks.

After crowns and other honours had been offered at Corinth, the remains were conveyed to Demetrias, a city to which Demetrius had given his name, peopled from the inhabitants of the small villages of **Iolcus**.

Postscript

Demetrius left two children by his first wife Phila, to wit, Antigonus and Stratonice; and two other sons, both of them named Demetrius; the one surnamed The Thin, by an Illyrian mother, and one who ruled in Cyrene, by Ptolemais. He had also, by Deidamia, a son, Alexander, who lived and died in Egypt; and there are some of say that he had a son by Eurydice, named Corrhabus. His family was continued in a succession of kings down to **Perseus**, the last, from whom the Romans took Macedonia.

Narration and Discussion

How did Demetrius' funeral rites mirror his life?

The surname or nickname given to Demetrius was *Poliorcetes*, meaning "Besieger," or in North's translation, "Fort-gainer." Do you think this name was well chosen? Can you think of a better one?

For older students: "For what better end can evil and unadvised kings and princes look for, of all their troubles, dangers, and wars? who indeed deceive themselves greatly, not only for that they follow their pleasure and delights as their chiefest felicity, instead of virtue and honest life: but also, because that in truth they cannot be merry, and take their pleasure as they would." Was this true of Demetrius?

Creative narration #1: Write a conversation between people in one of the towns as the funeral fleet passed by.

Creative narration #2: Complete the "family history project." What would Antigonus have to say about his father's life and ending, or perhaps about his own plans for the future?

Examination Questions

For Younger Students

1. How was Demetrius inspired by the example of his father Antigonus?

2. Describe a) the early life and career of Demetrius, b) his final days.

For Older Students

1. See (2) above.

2. (High School) Plutarch wrote: "So, in the same manner, it seems to me likely enough that we shall be all the more zealous and more emulous to read, observe, and imitate the better lives, if we are not left in ignorance of the blameworthy and the bad." Do you agree? How might this apply to the *Life of Demetrius*?

Bibliography

Plutarch's Lives of the Noble Greeks and Romans. Englished by Sir Thomas North. With an introduction by George Wyndham. London: Dent, 1894.

Plutarch's Lives: The Dryden Plutarch. Revised by Arthur Hugh Clough. London: J.M. Dent, 1910.

Made in United States
Orlando, FL
08 June 2024

47634187R00124